Songs to the Unsung

Cover artist: Lynda Bell, 'The Guardian'

SONGS *to* the UNSUNG

- an anthology of prose and poetry by -

KAYLEEN M. HAZLEHURST

Revised Edition published 2026
First published in New Zealand in 2023 by
Blue Dragonfly Press

National Library of New Zealand Cataloguing-in-Publication Data
Hazlehurst, Kayleen M, 2023
Songs to the Unsung/ Kayleen M. Hazlehurst

ISBN 978-0-473-66231-8 (International Edition)

Designed and distributed in New Zealand by
The Copy Press, 141 Pascoe Street,
Annesbrook, Nelson, 7011, New Zealand
www.copypress.co.nz

COPYPRESS

My love. Listen. Are you sleeping?

—John Updike, *The Centaur*

Contents

Introduction / 1

Between Auckland and the Bombays / 5
Earth Warriors and Pale Frogs / 7

Among the Cotton Tails / 9
Young Girl Waits / 16

The Gull / 19
A Distant Muting / 27
From Liquid to Light / 28

Cherry Sails / 31
Wild September Oranges / 44
A Weka waits for Breakfast / 45
Under the Ylang-Ylang Tree / 47

The Letter Home / 49
First Fall / 55
The Sidewalks of Montreal / 57

Farewell to Relics / 59
Old Cobbers / 76
Lamb and Latte / 78

Nora's Sword / 81
Come the Winter — 1918 / 91
A Spring Milking / 92

Safer Routes / 93
Three Poems — 1947 / 106

Louise / 109
Last Plane to Paradise / 136
King Tides / 138
The Citadel / 139

Ode to a Chestnut Tree / 140

Kayleen M. Hazlehurst

Introduction

Close to dawn one morning when I was about fourteen I had my first auditory dream. A great orchestra was playing a beautiful symphony, accompanied by a chorus of singers. I was so moved by this that I woke weeping. My distress was caused by an urgent sense that I should write this music down but, unlike Beethoven, I didn't have the skills.

As writers, artists or even politicians we can always keep an ear open to the music of the spheres. Our physical world may be impaired, but somewhere between belief and science there is a wonderful space for creative imagination. Here, we can reside and seek inspiration. Here, we can compose our own interpretation of experience. Over the years I have become convinced that even in the direst of circumstances we can keep on singing.

Poetry encapsulates our emotions in time and space—the vibrational qualities of sea, sky or forest, a special fall of light, the palpable effects of colour, sound and silence. And, of course, those profound questions that fire our convictions.

We read the poems of others for their familiarity and insights. We write poetry so we can revisit different eras and moments of contemplation. These scribblings sanctify places we want to recall, purify passions we may have long since outgrown, and enhance the compassion we have for our fellow creatures (and increasingly, for the planet). As antennae of a changing world, they can alert us to coming catastrophes and counsel us like wise friends.

Novels and stories have their own contexts and colours, their own journeys, star maps and visions. They explore new territories. They employ an ease of language that creates intimacy between the characters and the readers, until the very last page and beyond.

Songs to the Unsung is a selection of works by one New Zealand author that spans several phases from youth to adulthood. Visual images and themes, toyed with in earlier years, became pools of ideas for later prose and verse.

Contemporary Reflections: The joy of a road trip. Grief for a dying ocean. An experience of Covid quarantine. A warning about high tides and tyrants. A cross-dressing amateur detective and his failed sniffer dog gain acceptance in a small country town.

     Kayleen M. Hazlehurst

Kawau Island: A haunted girl longs for the return of her lover. A weka waits in the rain for his breakfast. Storms of love and loss are expressed in romantic language, interwoven with exotic landscapes—and other experiments.

Far from Aotearoa: A young man misses his family and gets into a pickle with a New York City policewoman. A lovelorn student is befriended by a squirrel among the 'wood and ices', the snowy roof-tops of Montreal.

Home and Country: A childhood ode to a chestnut tree. Seaside stories for young adults. Poems and ballads in memory of my father that speak of the beauty and sorrows of rural life.

Wartime: Passages from two novels and a short story about strange goings-on in a small Australian town are set in wartime. Although I was born in 1949, readers may sense an intimacy with the Second World War period in my work. The story-telling legacy endowed to me by my parents and grandparents is echoed here. It sparked in me many years of research and inspired my creative imagination.

There may be uncaught masterpieces or mislaid harmonies in our lifetimes, but eventually we *can* learn how to write the music down.

KMH

Between Auckland and the Bombays

Wild flowers line the highway
   between Auckland and the Bombays.
Moonstone, claret and magenta.
   Pigface, poppy and calendula.
They blur the peripheral senses,
on the expressway to the Waikato.

Here, a pilgrim chooses
   … coast or city grey?
Near Maggie's Grill and the Fruit and Veg,
   or the cabbage farm and the megalith.

Gliding down the Razorback
   … turning off at Pōkeno.
Past the bank of daisies,
   stopping off at the village for tea.

Whitebait fritters, shared with strangers.
   Lives portrayed in common waistlines,
common wallets, common dreams.
   United by an evergreen.

Against the silver clouds
    the heart of a hawk is beating.
He scans his living world,
    more deciduous than our own.
Winter's gossamer dreams and naked lace,
    with October buds appearing.

(*Up Flynn Road, across Cook Strait, through the Magellanic
Cloud*, Orplid Press, Hamilton, 2021)

 Kayleen M. Hazlehurst

Earth Warriors and Pale Frogs

Hydrangeas cover the door to the greenhouse.
Frogs come up the toilet. Pale things.
'Put down the lid,' you say, 'it will keep them out.'
I say, 'I've not seen them.'

I worry about bushfires.
You're surrounded by trees, cannot drive.
You say you can outrun a bushfire.
I say, 'Don't be silly, course you can't.'

A tsunami might hit the coast.
Exactly when, they're uncertain. Be prepared.
'Tidal waves' we used to call them.
Beset. Is this how our parents felt during the war?

You worry about dryness, the garden.
I keep an eye out for storms and floods.
Fish are drowning in a sea of plastic.
We're saddened. How can we help the fish?

I say people will learn to do better.
They will learn how to rescue the planet.
'Earth warriors' we used to call them.
You laugh and say, 'So we did.'

In the meantime …
Let's keep the toilet lid down.
Just in case pale frogs come to visit.
… 'Cup of tea?'

(Paradise Lost Series, 2019)

(Fresh Ink: A Collection of Voices from Aotearoa New Zealand, 2019,
Cloud Ink Press Ltd, Auckland, 2019, www.cloudink.co.nz)

   Kayleen M. Hazlehurst

Among the Cotton Tails

IN SOME PLACES the old coast road had dropped away. Last winter's rains had carved shallow gullies through the clay and sandstone, washing what was left of the gravel into narrow ridges of gunmetal against strips of pumice. Gusts of dry air toyed with dust and debris where water had once run.

Fallen trees covered with mosses and new growth saplings were familiar landmarks. The umbrella heads of ponga dissolved into the silver-grey of mānuka, while increasing numbers of shag and heron on inland ponds bore witness to the approaching coastline. A final burst through scrub brought them into an ivory expanse of dunes, cotton tails and other wild grasses.

Glass-fine sand under feet freed from jandals ensured that the last twenty yards of pathway to the beach house culminated in a celebration of the senses. The cry of seabirds, the pounding surf, the smell of seaweed—each strung, like so many more beads, into the awakening consciousness of girlhood and youth.

Unpacking was a kind of coming home. The companionship of travel had drawn the family closer. Irritation expressed in parents' voices during the hours of packing and 'getting away' was replaced by gentler tones of fond instruction. Children became co-operative and fleet-of-foot. Food and blankets, clothes and boxes, old rods and tackle were stashed in rightful places in readiness for holiday pursuits.

In the narrow kitchen their mother prepared an 'easy meal' of eggs and baked beans on toast, with hot Milo. On either side their father took charge of water-boiling manoeuvres, for feet and face washing in aluminium bowls retrieved from cupboards, and assigned to children on first nights, before the water tank heated.

Jamie and her twin flung themselves onto the bunks—Peter on top, she on the bottom—to bury their heads in the musty bedding. If the evening was inclement, hot water bottles would be tucked into sleeping bags, 'to expel the damp' their mother said. After lights-out, reading in bed was conducted by stealth and torch light among memories of summers past.

 Kayleen M. Hazlehurst

Before venturing forth to spots known to be fruitful, Dad would spend the morning untangling the tackle, muttering oaths over snarled lines and birds' nests abandoned the previous year. Mum would evict knots with her fingernails, threading new hooks and old sinkers onto lines of varying antiquity. Dad would be despatched bearing four lamb sandwiches, a cold sausage, a lump of cheese, an orange, and a packet of gingernut biscuits to dunk in his tea.

At mid-morning, Mum went to the beach for 'a refreshing swim'. Her sturdy turquoise swimsuit with its tummy support, skirted front piece and low-cut back, framed the pleasantly freckled flesh of her generation. Her sorties were undertaken with the minimum of provisions—a thermos of tea, a buttered scone, a paring knife and apple, a magazine, beach towel and bathing cap all stuffed into an old straw kit.

From dawn Peter was out in the bay in his iridescent togs with the older boys. From the balcony Jamie watched his slim torso, well-proportioned for a boy of thirteen, plummeting down the green water, spinning his board over spent foam, or paddling out to sea in search of another wave.

As children, Peter and Jamie had often lain among the cotton tails to spy upon the teenagers. The first days of summer were important in these rituals of friendship.

Beaches were dance floors, where girls in hip-hugging costumes giggled and posed, while boys displayed their surfing agility or threw themselves on the sand to flirt with the sisters of their friends.

Jamie longed to be a part of this, but her main wish was to see Johnny Allen again. After a quick orange juice, she tied a floral wrap around her waist, grabbed the largest towel, and ran towards the beach.

⤠

Someone was holding her hand. She could feel the plumpness of his palm, the softness of his fingers. He was holding and turning her hand, stroking each side. Lifting and kissing it, then placing it back down on the bed. It was her husband; she knew his energy. He was not happy.

There was a noise—a squeak of door, a shuffle of feet, a rustle of bag and coat being placed on the chair.

'How is she, Dad?'

'Not bad. Quiet, anyway.'

'Of course she's quiet, she's in a coma.'

'Maybe she can hear us. They say people can.'

'Wishful thinking. But if it helps, keep talking. It can't do any harm.' Her tone was condescending.

'It's *not* wishful thinking, Annelie. There've been studies. People wake up. *Why* are you so cynical?'

 Kayleen M. Hazlehurst

'I'm sorry. Let's not argue in case it upsets her.'

There was a sucking-in of air. A sob. A murmur of sympathy. Was he crying?

'Oh Dad, I'm so sorry.'

Please don't take your hand away, John. She remembered the crumpling of his face, the tremor in his voice when he first heard the news. Ovarian cancer. She was only fifty-two.

'Should I bring the kids in again, do you think?'

'No, Annelie. She's too unwell for the grandchildren. Let's give her some peace.'

That's right, dear. You be firm.

⚘

The sand dunes were covered with fluffy white tufts that shifted gently on olive-grey sprigs. Ocean grasses that had held the hills together against the years of tides and winds. She meandered down the trail. Soft sand made running difficult, requiring perseverance. A determined lifting of feet that sank deep with each footfall. Then there was an opening, a sloping away of the dunes. She had arrived.

⚘

Annelie had gone back to her office, back to her life. John was eating sandwiches from greaseproof paper and pouring coffee from his thermos. She was conscious of rustling and the smell of warm liquid. *I'm glad you're looking after yourself.*

The doctor came in, she recognised his heavy step. It was an appearance she dreaded. He took the chart from the bed, muttered something and replaced it with a 'clink'. The surgery had been radical, he warned, she might not recover. He was troubled by this unexpected decline.

'Mrs Allen, can you hear me?' The specialist lifted her eyelids, found nobody home, apparently, and left.

Friends were gathering on the beach. Talking. Laughing. Jamie held back. He emerged from the waves at the far end carrying a much larger surfboard. He had grown taller. The two years difference in their ages didn't matter.

She chose a spot halfway between them and lavishly spread out her towel, untied her wrap, and stretched out her bikini-fit body. It was important not to appear too keen. High school next year was co-ed, so they'd be seeing a lot of each other. Soon Johnny Allen would wander over and they'd talk about summer plans.

She sat up to examine the terrain. A ribbon of white

   Kayleen M. Hazlehurst

traced the coastline. The dunes flowed from the hills to the rippling edge of the shore. It was a favourite location for sunbathers. A tide-firmed beach was baking in the morning sun. By midday a crust would form on the surface to break at the touch into triangles and squares. All glistened—the ocean, the people, the sand—as if handfuls of fine crystal had been spread over everything.

His figure loomed in shadow above her. They chatted.

'Can I hold your hand this summer, Jamie?'

'Yes. That would be nice.'

He jumped, almost spilling his coffee. 'Did you say something, darling?'

He placed his ear close to her mouth.

'Hold my hand, Johnny,' she whispered. 'Hold my hand, always.'

(Shortlisted: Short Prose Section, *NZSA New Zealand Heritage Literary Award* 2021; Winner: 3rd place NZSA Northland Short Story Competition 2021, www.nzherald.co.nz/northern-advocate)

Young Girl Waits

She watches.
Craft skitter between the bays.
  Fishermen to fishing grounds.
Islanders to cribs. Lovers to hideaways.

Launches of the wealthily employed.
  Yachts of the determinedly idle.
Tackle and rods thrown among duffle bags.

Another silver fan departs.
Pōhutukawa necklace the sea cliffs,
  valiant roots reaching down
to banks of flax and wild agapanthus.

The ferry arrives.
People with banana boxes,
  dogs on leads, cats in cages
traverse the jetty, under the gimlet eyes of gulls.

The air lifts.
Caressing the cabbage trees,
  bringing out fantails, affable and teasing
with the scent of jasmine, oranges and wild tobacco.

     Kayleen M. Hazlehurst

She remembers the beauty of his stride.
Flame trees civilise the anarchy.
    The wild outer rim of mānuka,
curbed by hydrangea bushes and a rabble of geraniums.

She searches the horizon.
Gullies of ancient bushland shelter
    green-headed pigeons who banquet
on garden fruits and the rich dark berries of pūriri.

She lingers on the balcony.
Greying decks support palms and vines,
    yellow skins split open,
pulp scooped out by the ardent paws of possums.

She sleeps.
Weka haunt her evenings.
    In the valley strange ghosts are calling.
Her dreams laced with the soft white breath of pine.

When he returns she will welcome him—
    her hair blown silken across his skin.

(Kawau Island Series, 2009)

The Gull

A YOUNG WOMAN in jeans and windbreaker emerged from the red station wagon. She secured the leads on her excited dogs and was dragged by them to the beach, where they were released. Pulling up the hood of her jacket, she turned towards the Spit. Her sandshoes provided all the traction she needed for hopping from rock to rock until she reached the perimeter. There she braced herself against the diffusing spray, allowing the salty film to dampen her face.

She searched the rock pools for signs of life—casting about for periwinkles, shrimp and other sea friends. The spaniels adored this weekly treat of exploring the far end of the Spit. Jenny loved this volcanic outcrop with its irascible sea. Waves surged and thumped with a passion that stirred a poetic chord in her soul and at low tide there were always granite protrusions for Bunny and Pepper to clamber over.

Bunny, the gold and white spaniel, was the most daring. No dog pivoted skyward with greater joy than her. Pepper, the black and white, watched as her sister leaped into the water and climbed up new banks, avoiding them until she was sure they were safe. These adventures were profoundly soothing to canines. Jenny doubted anyone would find more well-balanced dogs.

Today, one dog was running lopsided. From a distance it was difficult to distinguish the white of the fur from the white of the feathers. As Bunny approached, triumphant as dogs are when they've found something special, Jenny saw that the dangling, flapping thing was a live bird.

After coaxing her pet closer, she grabbed the spaniel's collar and gently retrieved the trophy. It was a beautiful but very cross seagull. The wing was broken through, hanging together by threads of skin and sinew. Gulls took flight at the smallest provocation, so Jenny doubted it had been caught mid-air. Most likely, it had become tangled in fishing line. The wing had been shattered before the poor thing could break free. Bird injuries were common around this coastal region. Left on the rocks an injured gull would be fair game for any curious animal.

 Kayleen M. Hazlehurst

Jenny headed for the car, clutching the leads in one hand while suspending the furious seabird in the other. After reaching the vehicle, she wrapped the gull in a towel on the front seat and drove them all back to town.

The elderly vet always recognised a wildlife bundle and often allowed the rescuer to jump the queue at his clinic. There was a row of domestic patients in the waiting room—three cats, two dogs, and a rabbit. All eyes were upon the new arrivals.

'What have we here?' Dr Barnes lifted the edge of the towel.

'A seabird with a broken wing … Careful, he bites.'

'Another casualty of nature?'

'Bunny found him on the rocks.'

'Let's put him in a cage, shall we?'

Jenny bowed her head and followed the lab-coated man into a back room. An orange beak snapped at the vet's fingers as the gull declared his indignity at being unwrapped.

'He's quite big,' Jenny said, as the cage door clicked shut on the bird's last vestige of freedom.

'Hm-m-m. He's a southern black-backed gull.' Dr Barnes observed the bird through the bars. 'He'll have to be put down. Leave it with me.' He dismissed Jenny and returned to the waiting room.

She walked past the reception and back to her car, feeling ashamed. The seagull had trusted her and now she was abandoning him. A thought came to mind. *Maybe one of the younger vets could try mending the wing as an experiment, with pins and things.* She recalled the brave, cantankerous way the gull tried to defend himself, as if to say, 'I'm fine, thank you. Let me go, will you!'

The vet said this was the kindest thing to do. *What if the gull is permanently crippled? Do I really want a feral cat to attack him, or for him to die of starvation?* She searched her memory. *Wasn't there a wildlife sanctuary out on the Cape? Perhaps…*

She strode back into the office, sending another frisson of disturbance through the waiting room.

'I've come to take back the gull,' she announced.

Dr Barnes was holding a clinic folder. Beside him was a woman who looked annoyed. The practitioner removed his spectacles and examined Jenny from under his bushy eyebrows.

'You can't release him, you know.'

'Could the wing be pinned back together?'

'I'm sorry, we can only amputate at the break. Tidy it up a bit. The gull will never fly again.'

'Please save his life, Doctor. I'll pay for the surgery.'

 Kayleen M. Hazlehurst

She looked up at the vet with her most appealing smile.

His stern face softened. 'All right. I'll operate this afternoon. You can pick him up in a couple of days, but you must bring him back to me if he becomes sick. It's not fair on the bird.'

'I promise.'

⤜⤛

Three days later Jenny strode out of the clinic with a somewhat recovered, hissing gull in a box. Apart from looking odd, he was in good spirits and had been taking food. With the dogs left with a friend it was only Jenny and the gull heading along the dusty road towards Whale Breach Cape.

Winslow Cottage was a reminder of the diminishing viability of dairy farming, in a district yielding to growing demands for ocean views. The remaining twenty acres were enough to give it an air of elegant seclusion, without looking too forlorn. White peeling paint and bleached weatherboards were not untypical of farmhouses built in the early twentieth century. Yet amid the salt air and ocean winds, this cliff dwelling sat in a kind of stubborn contentment with its surroundings.

⤜⤛

An arthritic hand shifted the curtains as the station wagon negotiated its way up the steep drive. A woman watched the visitor reach into the car to take out a box. New charges induced in her a conflict of emotions. She was always ready to see any waif of nature in need of her protection but resented the human intrusion. She straightened her cotton shift and relaxed her face into a visitor's welcome as she opened the door.

The caller spoke from the foot of the steps. 'I hear you provide haven to the lost and the broken?'

This gentle enquiry warmed the widow. After introductions, they were soon on their knees examining the gull like fellow schoolgirls.

❦

Jenny asked the conservationist a torrent of questions about the sanctuary. She was hungry for stories about birds rescued and those returned to the wild.

'The amputation was severe, just below the joint, but it's healing well. Do you think he'll be all right, Mrs Winslow?'

The old woman tut-tutted as she scrutinised the surgery.

'Oh, yes. We have a large pen. He'll have plenty of company and will still enjoy the sea air. Some of our

 Kayleen M. Hazlehurst

residents are quite tame, you know. My husband and I converted the farm into a reserve long before caring for wildlife became fashionable.' She looked at Jenny, soft-eyed. 'You remind me of myself when I was your age.'

'I would love to help you,' Jenny said. Then, feeling her cheeks warm, she added, 'That is, if you need any help.'

Mrs Winslow sat back on her heels and smiled. 'We must give your bird a name.'

'Would "Bunny's Find" be appropriate?'

'It might be, if he were a racehorse.'

They both shrieked with laughter, frightening the bird into flapping his wing-and-a-half.

'How about Archie,' Jenny said. 'I assume it's a boy?'

'That would be easier to remember. Come, I will show you around. Have you ever thought of becoming a naturalist, dear?'

'I think I'm already a bit of a naturalist.'

Jenny followed the old woman through the back door, encountering an arrangement of pens on a grassy enclosure sheltered by a thick hedge. At the northern corner a domed aviary, the size of a small house, was being warmed by the sun. Inside, a motley collection of birds pecked at food being presented by a brown-haired caretaker. He deftly backed out of the enclosure and shut the gate as the two women approached.

'I'd like you to meet my grandson. He's studying to be an avian biologist,' Mrs Winslow said with pride. 'Archie likes to work here during his holidays, when he's not writing his thesis on the social life of seabirds.'

Jenny suppressed a squeak when she realised it was the same name she'd proposed for her gull. 'Glad to meet you Archie,' she said, extending her hand.

A young man with deep brown eyes and the warmest of smiles turned from the gate. As he offered his left hand in a greeting, Jenny saw that his right arm had been severed—just below the elbow.

(Young Adults, 2008)

 Kayleen M. Hazlehurst

A Distant Muting

Dark, the distant muting of the pines.

Ripple of willows at the creek.
    Last beat of wings.
Gums release their final acrid scent.

Spiders chase into evening nests.
    Gulls consort on singular stretch.
Tūī silence, until first new chill of day.

Moon's pale sash across the gulf.
    Light dispersing. Inlets making.
Capes, cast off from islanded floors.

Sight made clear by luminous eyes.
    Dew made ice, dissolves,
as boatmen slip into a feathery dawn.

Shimmer of sea …
    Bite of spray …

Nets heft hard against a sullen tow.
    Vessels befriended by gulls,
on the promise of a fishermen's breakfast.

(Kawau Island Series, 2008)

From Liquid to Light

A skein of silk,
   —ingathering mist,
fingers the forest,
   curdles the coast.

Once gnarly, once razor,
   the island peak,
now softened, now blended,
   with its sandy feet.

Once buoyant, once solid,
   the calloused reef,
embraced, at last,
   by the pallid deep.

Vessels and moorings,
   the ocean entire,
take flight in adoring
   a solitary sky.

Once shrouded …
   once whitened …
Once blended …
   once bleached…

 Kayleen M. Hazlehurst

The fingered forest,
    and the bladed peak.
The sandy footings,
    with their dull repeat.

Exposed again, comely,
    —so, abruptly, exposed.

A skein of silk—drifting.
    illumined veil—lifting.

My tempered sight—shifting
    from liquid to light.

(Kawau Island Series, 2009)

(Highly Commended, Margaret Reid Poetry
Prize for Traditional Verse, USA, 2009)

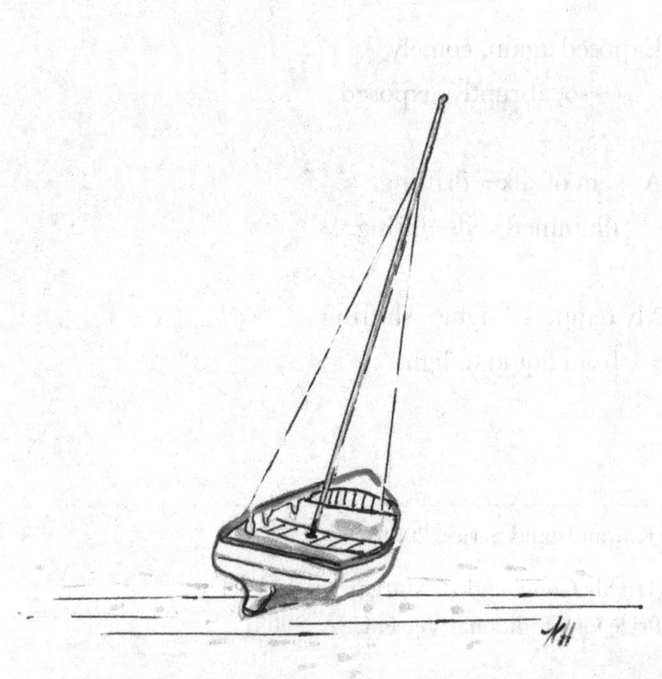

Cherry Sails

THE GIRL LOOKED over the quiet harbour. It had been ten days since the last rains and the still air was typical of the bright days of approaching summer. Birds hovered above her, resting their wings on currents of ocean air. The beach was yet undisturbed by early joggers and her morning walks to the point at the far end always rewarded her with some new wonderment.

Most of the fishing boats had left before dawn. White shapes dotted the sea like so many seabirds painted on a sapphire canvas. Nearby, other boats pulled against their moorings, lifting and bobbing against the roll of a morning tide. Each waiting to be set free.

White sandstone and clumps of ocean grasses provided nesting places for at least twenty varieties of gull. By taking the cliff path she could observe the birds tending to their cavilling young. The noise and energy generated by two or three balls of feathery down never failed to amazed her. Sleek, black-eyed parents fussed and stalked about their chicks, or swooped off in search of more food. Debbie would sit wedged between two rocks for over an hour, watching.

The point, this finger of rock jutting into the sea, was her favourite place to be. She liked to study the bluffs and bays of the distant islands. From here she could survey the coastal fringe of Queensland as it disappeared into a blue haze of gums and rainforest.

From the cliff top her future stretched out before her like the broad skyline. Time no longer mattered. She was free of timetables and exams. As a student, Debbie had been a little precocious, starting school at four-and-a-half and completing her final year at sixteen. Her family insisted there was no rush to make a decision about a career.

She arched her body into the wind as it swept up the cliff and ran invisible fingers over her face and hair. Everywhere there was the leafy-green scent of germination. Fragrances, wafting up from village gardens and shrubs, or from wild flowering vines and thickets of pawpaw and mangoes.

In March, she would begin an Arts degree at the University of Queensland and would see where that

    Kayleen M. Hazlehurst

led her. *If I spend a year sampling courses it won't matter*, she thought. *Maybe this will give me a chance to catch up with my schoolmates. Now it's summer I won't give study another thought.*

When she arrived at Nell Island Debbie had thrown her arms around the chubby necks of her mother's relatives the moment she stepped off the ferry.

'Aunt Dolly! Uncle Jim!' As a child she had spent many happy holidays in their company.

'My sweet love, how lovely you look,' said her aunt. 'What a pretty dress, and look at your long hair. Your mother was a chestnut at your age.'

Debbie blushed and looked around the wharf, hoping no-one was listening. Greeting relatives could be embarrassing, but she didn't really mind.

'I'll take those,' said Uncle Jim reaching for her suitcases.

'Thanks.'

'Come now,' said Aunt Dolly. 'Everyone to the car. Dinner is waiting and I'm sure you'll want to change into something cool.'

The locals considered it their duty to unravel guests from their city clothing and to get them into shorts. Debbie knew the routine and was expert at such transformations. She cast off her chrysalis of cares as she hung up her city dress and jumped into a tepid shower. In the morning she would go for her first walk and fall into the rhythm of island life.

'Are the fish biting, Uncle?' she asked over the roast lamb with minted peas, pumpkin and new potatoes.

'A few. Fish go north as soon as the outsiders arrive. Like ducks in hunting season, I reckon they know when it's time to take off.'

Last year she had snorkelled with the family on the Great Barrier Reef where marine life was protected. Uncle Jim believed the reef was where the local fish went in the summer.

'Yes,' she agreed. 'The fish in the marine parks are so tame. I've had orange roughies and blue-spotted cods take food from my hand. Even the eels were friendly, as long as you didn't threaten them.'

'Oh, my dear.' Aunt Dolly put a hand on her bosom. 'I'd be afraid they'd take off my arm. Now don't you listen to your Uncle's complaining, he does very well with his fishing. He takes out the boat every Wednesday, Friday and Sunday.'

'I would go fishing on a Tuesday if you'd join me.' He winked. 'Just give your old uncle the word. I'm always looking for an excuse to pull up the anchor.'

'Maybe in a day or two. After I've unwound.'

'That's right, darl'n' ... Don't you pester her, Jim. You

     Kayleen M. Hazlehurst

do as you please, Debbie. Shall we have a slice of my best pav? We can have it with a cuppa on the balcony.'

Aunt Dolly gathered up their dinner plates and went in search of three indulgent servings of pavlova with cream and strawberries, insisting she wouldn't hear of being helped.

Debbie sighed. 'Two wonderful months, Uncle. I can't tell you how much I've looked forward to this. I wish I could live here all year round.'

'You deserve a good holiday after your hard slog at school. Anything special you'd like to do this summer, apart from a bit of fishing?' He cast a sly glance in the direction of the kitchen.

'Some swimming and reading. Lots of walks. I thought I'd get a little waitressing at a restaurant. Two or three evenings for pocket money. What do you think?'

'I don't know much about the fancy restaurants, but there's a café on the waterfront that seems to be the favourite haunt of young people.'

'The Mudcrab?'

'Is that what it's called?' He laughed. 'Half the time I can't remember, they change their names so often.'

'Do you know the managers?'

'Afraid not. They're new. But you go down there and ask for a summer job, young Debbie. Give our address if you like. The number of years you've been visiting, you're almost a local.'

She liked that idea and *did* think of herself as an island girl.

Christmas on Nell Island was the season for ferries and water taxis. Debbie could relate to local feelings about these intruding mainlanders. They came with their noisy children and inquisitive ways, eating ice creams and dropping wrappers on the beaches and paths. The spaces around eateries became filled with the al fresco merriment of strangers.

The island was usually quiet in early December. The weather was mild and summer tourists had not yet arrived. It was Debbie's favourite time for long walks and introspection. In the evenings she liked to sit for an hour or two on the beach.

A ponytailed figure in rolled up jeans and T-shirt, with her knees drawn up to her chin, was barely noticed. She picked up another handful of the ivory grains and released them over her ankles and toes while vibrant colours, crimson and orange, cut swathes across the sky.

People were now tending to their last chores of the day. Boats were anchored or hauled up on the shore. Balls and frisbees, the earlier distraction of children and dogs, had given way to the slow movements and

     Kayleen M. Hazlehurst

low laughter of strolling lovers. *What will life be like for me a year from now?*

A flash of cherry red caught her attention. The bays and inlets of this region were a paradise for windsurfers and yachties. On a good day the harbour was full of tiny figures on boards or boats, attached to a palate of darting yellow, red, lime and tangerine. She saw a figure pulling in a small yacht at the water's edge. Although she enjoyed her solitude, she realised with surprise that she was lonely. High school was over. Her friends had gone their separate ways, perhaps for a lifetime, and she was missing their company.

The young man reached up to release a cord and his sails fell in graceful waves of rippling canvas—*fulup, fulup, fulup*—upon the deck.

Debbie stood to dust sand from her knees. Drawn by a desire to touch the beautiful cherry sails, she ambled down to the shore then stopped at a respectable distance.

He didn't look up. Instead he moved in fluid movements to bind the ropes and secure the sails. He was older than her, maybe in his twenties. Plainly, he was accustomed to outdoor life. His body was lean and toned. Shaped, her uncle would have approvingly said, like a man who was not afraid of a hard day's work. His fair hair and strong features were offset by a good tan.

On first impressions he was a typical Aussie surfer, except his sport of choice was sailing.

Debbie felt a sudden shyness. She had seen him before and realised she was staring. He reached into the bottom of the boat to pull out a duffle bag and looked up smiling.

'Hello,' he said, throwing the bag on the deck and dragging out an item of woollen clothing.

'Hi.' Her answer was so soft it was a wonder he heard her reply.

The cream rollneck jumper he'd pulled on hung loose over his jeans. The home-knit garment sagged at the corner where one hand had disappeared into a hip pocket. With the other, he picked up his bag and threw it on his shoulder.

He studied her more closely. 'Don't you waitress at The Mudcrab?'

'Yes. Wednesday and Friday nights.' Now she recalled where she'd seen him. During the week he had come into the café with a group of mates. Spoilt city boys. They had been a bit rowdy, although pleasant enough to her.

'What's your name?'

'Debbie Sutherland.'

'Jason Peters. Do you often come down to the beach in the evenings?'

'When I'm not working.'

'Okay ... Well, see ya round, Debbie.'

 Kayleen M. Hazlehurst

He strode off in the direction of the carpark without so much as a backward glance.

She didn't know why she felt cross, but she did. There were many things she would've liked to ask him—about the coast he sailed around and what he saw, how the sea changed colour at different times of the day, about his alluring cherry sails. Instead, she'd hardly spoken a word and Jason Peters didn't seem one for making conversation.

She started to walk home, watching her feet slide over the grass between the footpath and the road. *He thinks I'm just a kid. Well, little does he know.*

'Ah-h-h, I feel so stupid!'

On Friday evening Jason came back to the café with three friends. Debbie's heart gave a little skip. *Is this a double date?*

'Hi Debs. How're you doing?'

'Fine,' she said, in what she hoped was a dismissive tone.

He didn't bother introducing his companions. They, equally, showed no interest in their waitress. Later, standing in the shadows beside the bar, Debbie examined the 'girlfriend'. Like Jason, she was slim and tanned. The girl kept flipping her blonde hair and laughing prettily. Jason seemed besotted.

The four of them appeared to be university friends. She overheard them talking about their lectures, favourite pubs in Brisbane, and where the best music was playing on Saturday nights. Jason was doing an Engineering Degree. The girlfriend was studying Law. *An ideal couple?*

During the evening the students were tolerably well-behaved, lingering after dinner over coffee. At eleven o'clock closing, they left.

Debbie took evasive action, deciding to avoid the beach. The next morning, she ventured forth to the point accompanied by one of Aunt Dolly's famous packed lunches—egg salad sandwiches with baby tomatoes, orange juice and two cornflake biscuits. She took the slower route around the rocks, arriving at the cliff path by lunchtime. The rest of the afternoon she spent on the cliff top gazing over the ocean and watching the birds.

Today the sailboats were out in numbers and she strained to pick out his yacht. Once she thought she caught a glimpse of his cherry sails against the sparkling water and felt her heart calling out to him.

Don't be ridiculous, Debbie, she told herself. *You hardly know the guy.*

The managers had phoned to ask if she would take an extra shift. Saturday evenings were always busy, they

 Kayleen M. Hazlehurst

said. That night Debbie started work with a strange mixture of dread and longing. It was a feeling she'd never experienced before. By nine there was still no sign of him and she had begun to relax, when he arrived.

He came in quietly, drawing up a stool at the bar and ordering a beer. From his clothes, she could see he'd come in straight from the bay. He was wearing that old cream jumper Debbie was becoming distinctly fond of. She admired the sinewy line of his sockless ankles between the tattered sandshoes and turned-up cuffs of his jeans. This time she decided she would take the initiative.

'Your friends are not with you tonight?' she asked, as she wiped down the surface of the bar.

'Hi Debs. No, I'm all alone. Sad, isn't it?' He grinned.

It was a gorgeous smile. His amused grey-blue eyes reminded her of Uncle Jim's when he was up against Aunt Dolly.

'So, where's your girlfriend?' she asked, feigning indifference.

'My girlfriend! Hardly. At least not as far as Jennifer is concerned.'

Oh, he's disappointed. He must like her a lot. 'Maybe she'll come back.'

'Not until the New Year. Gone to Brisbane to buy up the town before Christmas. Will you join me for a drink, Debbie?'

Should she? She polished even harder. He reached out to stop the motion of her forearm, and his touch sent a shock of electricity through her body.

'Please, Debs. I could do with a friend.'

She struggled to answer such an appealing request for her company. 'Maybe later.'

'When do you finish work?'

'I'm off at eleven.'

'Great. I want to know all about you.'

'My, what big eyes you have Grandmama,' Debbie shot back, startling even herself.

For a second their eyes locked. He flicked back his head under the invisible blow and let out an injured howl, then they both collapsed with laughter.

'I promise to keep my bushy tail to myself,' he said, wiping mock tears from his eyes. 'Cheeky girl.'

After a long orange juice, he offered to walk her home.

'As long as we don't take too long. My Aunt and Uncle will be worried.'

'You're Aunt and Uncle? Hey, how old did you say you were?'

'I didn't.'

'Next year is the big one for you, eh? I guess you will be letting down your hair once you get to university.'

'Depends what you mean. I already have it pretty good.'

   Kayleen M. Hazlehurst

'Mm-m-m.' He turned Debbie to face him outside her gate. 'You're just a baby, aren't you,' he whispered, looking down.

She became conscious of how slight she was against his tall, solid frame, but when he pulled her into a gentle hug the years between them melted away. The smell of sheep's wool and salt stirred her senses. His hand swept over her forehead, brushing aside the chestnut fringe.

With one finger he raised her bowed head. 'This is where I leave you. We don't want to give your people a turn.' He looked into her silent face, as if making a decision. 'Would you like to come sailing with me tomorrow? We could take a picnic and go to the other side of the island. There's a nice beach there for swimming.'

'I'd like that. Come to the house in the morning. You can meet my family. I'm sure they'll like you.'

'Thanks for the vote of confidence. I'll pick you up at nine-thirty. Cheerio.'

He gave her a quick peck on the cheek and disappeared into the shadows of their narrow street.

(Young Adults, 1992)

Wild September Oranges

Crescent wings
  cutter through the drifts.
Lapis shadows
  gliding through the day.

Winter torrents
  yield to slanting mists.
Tears borne up
  by wings between the bays.

Wild September oranges,
  scent embracing near.
Reminiscent
  of other September partings.

Three storms pass.
  We ask the Earth for reasons.
And Earth replies
  by sending softer seasons.

(Kawau Island Series, 2009)

(Highly Commended, Margaret Reid Poetry Prize for
Traditional Verse, USA, 2009; Transformation, 2022
Anthology, Poetica Christi Press, Montrose, Victoria 2022)

A Weka waits for breakfast

A weka waits in the rain
    for his breakfast.
Supplies are running low.

Instead of tinned sardines
    it is instant noodles.
Cheap rations left by transient visitors.

The weka eats chaotically.
    Leaves half on the ground.
Inevitably, he will return to polish it off.

I reflect on island morality.
    No-one is completely honest.
There are degrees of duplicity and benevolence.

The locals are modest.
    Silence punctuates conversations
as much as contention punctuates the television.

Stark honesty is thought impolite,
    or at times downright unfriendly.
Truth is served favourably garnished, never raw.

The spare wood from under my bach
   is likely to disappear.
'Donated' by me to someone who needs it more.

A word of enquiry about its removal
   is met with an eye glazed
towards the sea and the mention of a good day's fishing.

(Kawau Island Series, 2009)

     Kayleen M. Hazlehurst

Under the Ylang-Ylang Tree

The jetty is empty now.
    Gone the evening swims
        that once revived you.

Your vigour has left you.
    A candle blown.
        A receded, iridescent tide.

You are at my shoulder again.
    I feel a tremor of energy,
        a current … a pulse.

I reach out for you,
    absorbed as a lover
        in your ethereal presence.

I float in your essence,
    we speak together
        of unkind separation.

We lay under the ylang-ylang tree,
    heady aromatic breaths
        renewing our will to live.

(Kawau Island Series, 2009)

(Highly Commended, Margaret Reid Poetry
Prize for Traditional Verse, USA, 2009)

The Letter Home

J EREMY SITS MORIBUND at his desk. He lowers his head of brown hair until his fringe falls forward. He rubs his eye sockets with the balls of his palms. For some reason this ritual helps with problems. For a young Kiwi on his own in New York there seem plenty of these. The particular problem at hand is to finish a letter home to his family in Aotearoa New Zealand.

'You'd think I'd have something to say after three weeks, but I've got bugger all.'

He hasn't met any girls to speak of and his social life is non-existent. He wants to look at universities, but nothing has gelled. Mostly, he reads and walks about the city exploring. He fingers the brochure of an IT college. *I'll check it out.* He wishes he could work. Anywhere, to meet people. *Washing dishes. Helping in the kitchens.*

'I should have gone to London for my big OE. At least they welcome Kiwis in British pubs and restaurants.'

He stretches his lanky legs under the table and raises his clenched hands above his well-formed shoulders. *Time to get back to the gym.* He misses the training, the weekly rugby matches, and his routine of weekend bicycling along the shoreline and through the forests of the Rodney District.

'I'll go mad if I don't get out soon.'

Fitness is a necessity for a bloke like him. His oxygen.

'Coffee!'

He gets up, prepares a cup and comes back to the desk. Slinging his right leg over his left knee, he rubs his blonde hairy calf and picks at his toes. He begins to write. At last he has added a few more words that should satisfy his mother. Dad and the girls wouldn't mind what he tells them.

Jeremy looks around. The apartment is a charmer. Quiet and warm. A nice leather couch, comfortable chairs, good internet connection. There are three large bay windows overlooking a park. Ten minutes to the shops and cafés.

His sister's boyfriend lent him the accommodation in exchange for his own flat near Auckland University. A kind of house-cum-holiday exchange. *A winter in New York ... Sounded good.*

    Kayleen M. Hazlehurst

He gazes out the window to the street below. Four o'clock, and already it's getting dark. Having done his duty, he seals the envelope and decides to slip out to the mailbox on the corner. *Then a bit of TV.*

Jeremy tears down the staircase with his letter. He doesn't bother putting on his coat, or his track pants, or even his jandals. It's a short walk to the corner. The large apartment door slams behind him. The pavement snow has worn thin. Crusty and grey from a thousand footsteps that day. He gets to the mailbox and is about to drop in his letter, when he is accosted by THE VOICE.

'HEY! WHAT YOUSE DOING?'

'Eh?' He jumps and turns around to be confronted by a short, rotund figure of the New York City police. A woman of senior years.

'I SAYS, WHAT YOUSE DOING?' repeats the figure of authority, flicking back her head.

'Posting a letter, Miss,' says the well-mannered country boy, feeling a little uncertain. 'Then I'm going back inside,' he adds quickly in case this helps.

'Youse going INSIDE, boy?'

'Yes, officer?'

'Just where INSIDE do you think youse going?'

'Over there.' Jeremy points to his apartment building, a couple of metres away.

'You don't live in THAT building?'

'Yes, I do,' he squeaks.

'You … do … NOT!' The officer waves her head from side to side in rhythm with her words.

'I do so.'

The figure puts her hands on her hips in exasperation, displaying evidence of a gun. 'You can't tell me you live there.'

'Why not?' Jeremy asks in a small voice.

'Cos, look at you. You got no clothes on. I ain't seen no one like you around here.' She lifts her radio to her lips to call backup.

'But I do-o-o-o.'

'Why you wear'n no pants?'

'I AM wearing pants. Look!' Jeremy gestures to his boardies. 'I'm wearing shorts.'

'You got no shoes on, an' it's winter.'

'U-m-m-m … I'm a Kiwi?'

'Say what?'

'I'm a Kiwi … It's our national dress?'

There is a long pause as the woman sizes him up. She checks around for the hidden camera or laughing colleagues. Is this a nutter or is he plain simple?

'I ran out to post a letter. I wasn't expecting to be out for very long. I forgot my keys. But I'll ring the bell for the concierge to let me in.' He moves towards the door.

 Kayleen M. Hazlehurst

'STAY… AWAY … from the apartment building,' orders the officer with her hand on the gun.

Jeremy freezes, mid-motion. 'But I live there, and I'm starting to get rea-l-l-y cold.'

He's now conscious that his summer shorts and bare feet are attracting public attention and the officer is enjoying the limelight.

'You live in a cardboard box more like,' snaps the officer.

There is a long pause.

'Are you all right there?' It is the voice of a pretty girl with long black hair who has arrived on the steps of the apartment building, poised with a key.

Sweet-as, Jeremy rejoices privately. 'Yeah, see. That's my neighbour.' He doesn't know the girl's name but they have said hello in passing. He straightens his shoulders and turns back to the mother-of-all-officers to check her next move.

'You know this man?' The officer moves begrudgingly forward.

'Oh, yes. He lives next door to me.'

The officer becomes fussy and official, following them into the lobby. She takes down everyone's name—the half-naked offender, the girl, the concierge—and turns with distaste to the resident. 'I suggest you take better care of your *friend*. An' see that he's dressed right.'

Jeremy smiles weakly, quiet as a lamb. The girl flicks him an amused glance. His eyes reply with a pained apology.

'I certainly will, officer.'

'Hawrumph.' The policewoman turns away, the corners of her mouth twitching.

After offering profuse gratitude and the exchange of names, Jeremy stumbles back into the apartment seeking out lights. Crumpled in his sweaty palm is his letter home. He sits down to smooth it out on the table. Taking his pen, he adds a few words. *I have just met the nicest girl next door.*

(Winner: Novice Award: *Rodney Writes
Short Story Competition,* 2009)

 Kayleen M. Hazlehurst

First Fall

This morning I woke in silence
    innocent of Nature's face.
Arose and glanced
    to see her smiling at me,
      white-haired in satin lace
with the wisdom of the year
    upon her shoulders.

Even the eaves and chimneys,
      red and ugly,
now, are Christmas colours,
      white and red.
Frosted and iced,
    tipped and gilded,
with the freshest flakes.

I will not hear the footsteps
    of the hungry squirrel
who befriended me this fall.
    Now muted, fat and curled
within his burrow for the final season.
    Winter, like a loving friend,
wraps her blanket over my shoulders.

We sit together, over tea,
remembering the lifetime of the year.
      Satisfied with the movements of birds
          that flit contentedly
            on wood and ices.
Warmth and sorrow, birth and death
          between their toes.

(Canada, 1976)

 Kayleen M. Hazlehurst

The Sidewalks of Montreal

Baked into the sullen earth,
    leaves imprinted upon sidewalks.
My memories of sweet, grey rocks.
    Grey and dreary rocks,
        sweet with the hush of wind jackets.
Cold lips and clouded breath.
Your chest surrounded me, that day.
    Warmth protecting against the
        vacuumless-vacuum that men create.
When we became each other's mitts and
    mukluks against the Arctic cold.
        Cold, though not unloved,
            but lonely were those spaces.
My feet pass daily now,
    under the watchful guide
        of eyes that look not up to see
you staring fair and golden from
    every head and beard …
Fair and golden as the leaves.
    Gone and golden as the leaves.
        Each one passes.

Oh, it is more peaceful to stare
　　at the leaves imprinted like memories.
At the memories imprinted like leaves
　　upon the sullen earth.
　　　　The sidewalks of Montreal.

(Canada, 1976)

　　　Kayleen M. Hazlehurst

Farewell to Relics

WALLY HEINZ EXTRACTED a long machete from the broken wall and held it up to the light. Much of the blade was mottled brown and orange. The bone handle, elaborately carved, was bound with the tattered remains of plaited cane. It was a fearsome looking instrument, about the length of a man's arm and sharp enough to catch glints from the sun.

The square-faced policeman looked down from the balcony.

'What the bloody hell do ya think you're doing?' he shouted. People were always trying to park on the double yellow line in front of his station. This time it was young Shane, the odd-jobs boy from the Heinz hotel.

'Sorry, sergeant. Mr Heinz sent me. Asks if you would stop in at his office.'

'Notice what was for lunch?'

'Eh?'

'Never mind. Now remove that truck before I give you a ticket!'

'Okay, chief.'

Frank Wilcox was a man who spoke plainly. His blood pressure danced to his emotions, both displayed in the reddening of his face. Like all the old-family geriatrics of this town, the sergeant was as solid as the local war memorial, although chiselled from a younger stone. He had won the reputation of being a damned good detective over the past twenty years—and these locals had long memories, some going as far back as the Mandalay murders of November 1946.

One of the more senior residents of Toonawanda, Arnie Chisholm, had an opinion on the matter. 'Why would anyone want to kill three of the best young fellas come back from the war? Hadn't they been through enough in Burma, without finding themselves knocked off on arrival?'

'They were hardly dead on arrival, now were they Arnie?' Wilcox remembered answering. 'It happened several months later, as I recollect?'

The Mandalay case was one of New South Wales'

 Kayleen M. Hazlehurst

great unsolved mysteries. Simpson, Pierce and Grant, who'd each survived as prisoners of war, were brutally slaughtered in their home town. Their hacked-up bodies were discovered buried beside a lake, five miles north of MacKinney's station. They never found all of the parts.

Spared certain death in the swamps near Mandalay, the servicemen had made a miraculous escape from the Japanese prison camp just before the end of the war. After being discharged from a Sydney army hospital, they returned to Toonawanda to take up fencing and farmhand work. The police never identified their killer, or even a motive. In 1955 investigations on the Mandalay case were closed.

'The whole town was in an uproar,' Arnie told Wilcox over a pint, not long after his posting in 1979. 'Those three blokes were well liked, sergeant. If you want to make ya'self famous, try solving that one.'

'As if I don't have enough to do chasing young buggers in fast cars and rescuing wives from inebriate husbands,' Wilcox had growled. There was no way he was going to let on that the case interested him. Especially not to a gossipy old bugger like Arnie.

Wilcox poked his grinning face around the door of the

publican's office. It was a room on the second floor, seldom seen by guests, with a red rug covering the hardwood floor.

'Well, what is it? More trouble with drunks and disappearing lodgers?'

'I wish. Come in, come in.'

They were old acquaintances. Wally Heinz was a calm contrast to his excitable city friend. Now in his mid-fifties, the publican had that composed demeanour suitable for a man who had spent a lifetime behind a bar.

'As long as I'm not kept from my flamin' lunch,' Wilcox answered in mock belligerence.

'I'll have it sent up. Will that be shepherd's pie or shepherd's pie?'

'Do I have a choice?'

'Nope.'

Heinz would turn out thirty drunks in a rainstorm and fear no consequences, but as he telephoned downstairs with the lunch order there was a tremble in his voice that made the sergeant suspicious.

'I've got something to show you, Frank.' The publican reached down to withdraw the exotic weapon. 'Don't know what to make of it.' He placed the handle of the pitted machete on the table, with the blade parallel to his head.

'Gawd Almighty, where did you find that?'

'Top floor, out the back. We've been knocking

 Kayleen M. Hazlehurst

down walls to make bigger rooms up there. Discovered this thing wedged between the two-by-fours behind a wardrobe.' He gave the weapon to the policeman.

Wilcox rolled the machete between his palms for a minute then pushed it back across the desk. 'What do ya want me to do with it?'

'That's not all we found.'

There was a quiet knock at the door. Nancy, the housekeeper, was ushered in with a tray of steaming mince with mash and peas and a cup of tea. She placed the tray on the desk in front of the sergeant.

'Thanks Nance.' Wilcox waited for her to leave. 'Don't play silly beggars with me Wally. What else have you got?'

The publican indicated to a black box on the desk. The lock and tin siding had already rusted away.

The sergeant lifted the box and gave it the once-over. He took out his pocket knife and poised the blade above the latch. 'Want me to open it?'

'Go ahead.'

He gave the latch a flip and the box disintegrated in his hands. Inside was a bundle of yellowed papers tied up with faded pink string. 'Love letters?'

'Could be government. They used pink tape.'

Wilcox laid the papers on the table between them so they could speculate on their contents.

'Handwritten,' observed Heinz, flipping through. 'Don't let your meal go cold.'

'Yeah, well.' He leaned towards his raised fork. 'Everyone handwrote in those days.'

'So why were they stashed in my hotel with that machete … and a finger?'

Wilcox choked back his mouthful of peas. After a coughing spate and a round of swearing he found his voice. 'Are you telling me there was a *severed* finger in that hole in the wall?'

Heinz cringed. 'Yeah, sorry. Looks like the remains of a finger. Could be a sheep's knuckle, for all I know.'

'Find a decapitated head in there too?' he shouted.

'No. Just a finger … or a knuckle. Keep it down, Frank, you'll frighten the staff.'

'Maybe someone didn't like your hot dinners!'

'Well, they weren't throwing *my* food behind wardrobes before 1967. Those letters are much older than that.'

Wilcox waved his palms downwards. 'Okay, mate. Show me where ya found this stuff. Where's this finger anyway?'

'Bones.'

'Bones, then.'

⊷

 Kayleen M. Hazlehurst

Forensics wasn't in a hurry to examine an old machete for traces of blood and hair for murders committed over fifty years ago, and it was going to take time to decipher a bunch of blotchy old papers. But at least the case was reopened and Sergeant Frank Wilcox was put in charge of local inquiries. When confirmed the bones were definitely the remains of a human finger the local newspaper took up the story. *Mandalay Murder Mystery. New Evidence Uncovered.*

'Did you know the hotel owners after the war?' the sergeant asked Arnie. He'd been interviewing all the old codgers in town.

Arnie thought for a minute. 'That would be the Chisholms.'

'I thought *your* family were the Chisholms?'

'That's right.'

'Flip'n heck. Your father owned the hotel?'

'Uncle.'

'Where were you at the time?'

Arnie regarded him with his filmy blue eyes. 'You'd be talk'n about the time of the murders, Mr Wilcox?'

'Yeah, about November 1946.'

'I was out shearin' that summer. Remember it well. When I got back the whole town was—'

'Yes, yes. I know, in an uproar … Didn't you go to war?'

'Flat feet.' The old man looked down at his worn

leather boots. The cuffs of his charcoal trousers were thick with dust and sweat.

The sergeant was aware of that pungent odour associated with octogenarians, and asked, 'You were around town the whole time?'

'When I wasn't out roustin' or shearin'.'

'Arnie, we came upon some mighty peculiar items stashed behind the wall on the top floor of the hotel.'

'I heard.'

'As I see it, there could be a connection between those items and the murders. Do you know who might have put them there?'

Arnie scratched his white bristles with blackened fingernails. 'Could have belonged to Eddy Porter.'

The sergeant took out his notebook and adopted a patient tone. 'So, tell me about Eddy Porter.'

'He worked for my uncle after he got back. Mighty funny bloke, Eddy. War did him in. A bit older than the rest.'

'You knew him well?'

'Everyone knew everyone round these parts.'

'Were ya *mates*, Arnie?' Wilcox's shoulders lifted and fell with his sigh.

'We was ankle-biters together. Yeah, we used t' yarn, though he never talked about the war. Sometimes he'd show me his things.'

 Kayleen M. Hazlehurst

'What things?'

'Old bits and pieces. Copper dishes from Cairo, clay pots from Malaya, wood carvings from New Guinea, china from London, old bullets, tin cups, buttons, diaries. Rubbish he'd swapped with other Diggers. He became a bit of a collector after the war.'

Avid collector of war memorabilia, jotted down the sergeant, pausing to check his spelling. 'Did you see a Japanese machete among those things, by any chance?' he asked innocently.

'Not as I recall.' Arnie was watching him with reptilian stillness, waiting for the next question.

Wilcox moved on. 'Where did he keep all this stuff?'

'Had it laid out on a table in his room. More like an altar, if you ask me.'

'Where *was* his room Arnie. Can you recall?'

'The staff lived in poky little rooms upstairs. Eddy loved his room. "At least it's my own", he used to say. I reckon he hoped some sorry female would look after him in return for china from London and bits of copper from Cairo. Silly bugger.'

'He never married?'

'Not that I heard. Left town about '56, or thereabouts.'

Suspect left town after the case was closed, noted Wilcox.

'Now, Arnie. I want you to think long and hard. Can you show me the approximate location of Eddie's room?

They've moved things around a bit since then.'

'S'pect so, as long as there's still a winda to look out.'

Wilcox gave a sad nod. Old countrymen had anti-quated skills. The position of a thing was ascertained by its relative distance from known landmarks—hills, rivers, clumps of rock, buildings. Skills useful during wartime. You wouldn't have thought it was 1999.

Arnie cast the silent policeman a sideward glance. 'You want me t' show ya now?'

'Tomorrow will do, round lunchtime. I've got a few things I need to check.'

'Awright,' the old-timer struggled up from the wooden chair and shuffled towards the door.

'And Arnie,' Wilcox called after him.

The old man turned to look back. 'Yeah?'

'Why didn't you tell the police this at the time?'

'Nobody asked.'

Harry Turner, a volunteer at the Australian War Memorial in Canberra, had jumped at the opportunity to assist when he received Frank Wilcox's phone call. The prison camps of Burma fared large in this living memorial to human endurance and sacrifice. There wasn't much Harry couldn't find out with a bit of research in the collections.

 Kayleen M. Hazlehurst

Two weeks later a brown paper parcel arrived by Australia Post. Turner confirmed that the Mandalay three who were murdered, along with Eddy Porter, had been in the same unit when they were captured in September 1944. Conditions at the Shimo Songkurai Camp were appalling. A medical officer recorded the agony of those days—the preciousness of an hour's survival. Reduced to three ounces of rice a day, the prisoners were dying in large numbers from starvation, exposure and beatings. Few escaped.

Constable Travis, the station junior, tracked down Eddy at an old people's home in North Sydney. Ravaged by ill health and alcohol, the eighty-seven-year-old wasn't worth much by the time he was interviewed. Questioning induced unintelligible ravings. There was no sign of an alleged hoard of war relics under his bed or among his meagre belongings.

Back at the station, the sergeant was confounded. Eddy Porter was their man, he was sure of it, but virtually the whole town had provided Eddy with an alibi. He'd been working at the pub at the time, they all claimed. Wilcox had other ideas. *Eddy must have kept that evil looking machete and severed finger. Couldn't help himself, could he? Couldn't say farewell to his dusty old relics, so he'd shoved them into the wall.*

Forensics reported the machete had been wiped clean.

The owner of the finger was untraceable, and the papers were a mixture of love letters and fragments of diaries. Perhaps they really were wartime tokens gathered by a damaged man trying to preserve the dreams of his dead mates.

One incident, recorded in barely legible pencil, stood out:

> Gee these Japs put the wind up you. One bloke ducked off from the work gang to the dunny without permission. When he came back this little guard slapped him across the face. Well, this Digger hauled off and decked him one. Pretty soon the other guards were swarming over him. At night we heard his screams and at roll call the next morning we saw they'd stuck him in a bamboo cage. An example to the rest of us. One day they took our fellow off into the jungle. Two guards with shovels. We never saw any of them again. That poor bugger copped it thick, I reckon.

This set Wilcox to brooding. Imagine the level of mateship between those survivors. Their codes of honour. What if someone was crossed? Some incident of cowardice with horrific consequences? To be slain so violently with an

          Kayleen M. Hazlehurst

enemy weapon and buried in the backblocks of New South Wales smelled to him like an execution. *Was this a symbolic act? Rough justice? Revenge?*

'Maybe a machete wielding Jap followed them back to Australia?' Constable Travis offered, unhelpfully.

'Son, you've been reading too many comics.'

At the end of the day the sergeant put down his spectacles.

'Ah, bugger it!' *What would their boys know about unholy revenge? Ordinary country lads most of them, trying to stay alive. Poor blighters.*

The love letters, the diaries, the relics—they were all irrelevant. Cast-off leaves in the winter of our humanity. Messages sent upon the winds to loved ones by the dying, or the soon-to-be-dead. Some were picked up and saved by sentimental blokes like Eddy Porter. This case was too cold. Whoever was responsible for the Mandalay murders would have come to grief years ago.

'I need a drink.'

The statement echoed around the stone office and holding cell. Everyone had already left the police station.

Outside the hotel dining room two elderly residents sat in their country bests, anticipating an evening at the local establishment. Their crushed-tobacco faces observed the world with a kind of clement irony. At five thirty they noticed Frank Wilcox making his way down the street towards the pub.

'Ya reckon he knows what he's doin', Fred?'

'Don't rightly know, Jack. This detective work might've gone to his head?'

'Old Tom says too much thinkin' can drive a man bonkers.'

'Is that right?' Fred turned in unhurried surprise towards his companion for explanation.

'Yep. Heat and thinkin' and the lack of a cold beer can drive a man mad in the bush.'

Fred clenched the remains of a cigarette between his yellowed teeth. 'Well, Tom oughta know. He reckons he's never done a day's thinkin' in his life.'

They both laughed.

At eighty-five, Tom had remarried a woman half his age and still rode his horse every day over the family property.

Jack nodded towards the meandering sergeant. 'This case he's got. It not a mystery, really. It's more of a quandary.'

'What's that when it's at home?'

'My Bertha was always getting herself into a quandary.' Jack often referred respectfully to his deceased wife.

'Yeah?' Fred queried, suitably impressed.

'Somewhere between a pickle and a problem, is a quandary.'

They gave a moment's silence to the plight of the country policeman with his unsolved case.

'Pity about poor Eddy,' Jack went on. 'After the war, he went mad with a machete. Threatening people. That's why they sent him away. Mind you, quite a few blokes did.'

'What, went mad with machetes?'

'Nah, only Eddy did. Poor bugger. The rest of them just went mad quietly.'

Fred examined his boots.

Jack softened his voice. 'Eddy told me once the Japs had him caged up like a dog. He blamed them three for it. Instead of saving him they used the ruckus to get away.'

Fred nodded towards the nearing policeman. 'Think he'll ever figure it out?'

'Not unless someone puts him out of his misery.'

Fred turned to Jack with a slow smile. 'So, ya reckon our sergeant has a quandary, then?'

'Yep. That would be it.'

Wilcox reached his destination. The one and only watering hole in Toonawanda.

'Looks like you need a pint, mate,' said the two in unison.

'Too right,' answered the policeman as he swept into the pub.

Jack and Fred staggered to their feet and dusted themselves down.

'I guess it's about that time,' said Fred, looking sufficiently elegant.

'They say he got away too, you know. Killed two guards with his bare hands.' Jack opened the hotel door graciously for his friend.

'Who got away?'

'Old Tom MacKinney.'

'Huh, I never heard that.'

'Nah, keeps hisself to hisself, old Tom.'

Fred stopped in wonderment, halfway between the world of dust and flies and the world of a nice cool pint and a rump steak. A few men inside looked up, bat-like, at the glare of daylight.

'How did that happen?'

'Japs were about to do in a mate. Tom tracked the 'em through the jungle. That's how he lost his finger.'

'Tough old bugger.'

The Heinz hotel door swung soundlessly behind them.

(Australia, 2000)

 Kayleen M. Hazlehurst

Old Cobbers

‘Get-away-back, Scotty.
　　Get-away-back, I say.’
‘Nah! Ya mongrel!
　　Not the scrub!’

‘Get-away-back, boy.’
　　Round up the sheep.
We’ve ten mile to drive ’em
　　Over rough, over steep.

‘Away-back there, Scotty.’
　　Loyal to a fault.
My partner, my workmate.
　　My old kelpie dog.

‘Get-away-back, old matey.
　　There’s a good lad.’
Get along home now,
　　Your work here is had.

There’ll be sheep there to gaze at,
　　and cows, so I’m told.
With blue skies till sunset,
　　and we’ll never grow old.

　　Kayleen M. Hazlehurst

No tax man to chase us,
    No banks to foreclose.
We'll amble sweet pastures,
    in our best Sunday clothes.

So, my old Scotty,
    My cobber-in-arms.
Make way for your master,
    I'm tired of this farm.

'Get-along, will ya!'
    Why lie there instead?
'There are paddocks to run in ...'
    Why green soaked with red?

'Get home now, old fella ...'
    No pain to be stood.
'I'll follow ya soon ...'
    As an old soldier should.

But just now, I'll rest
    on the butt of my gun.
'Oh Scotty, old friend!'
    With my tears flowing down.

(In memory of my father, 2008; *Scrub Anthology*,
Mansfield Readers and Writers Inc, Victoria, 2025)

Lamb and Latte

A Ballad to Jack and others

Up among the pastures
    you'll find our brother Jack,
with thirty feet or more to lay,
    if the fence don't break his back.

Phil has gone to get the cows,
    young Tom will help him too.
It's hard when Dad's a milking man,
    and you're ten and still at school.

Now it's not the bleakness or despair.
Nor drought, nor overdraft.
But cold envy of the mouths we feed
that breaks a farmer's heart.

Mum's built like a battleship,
    which is just as well, at that.
She'll knock ya flat if ya misbehave,
    then mend ya with her cake.

Pete, poor bloke, is short a few,
    it's kinder to be said.
He's been our valued general hand,
    since Bell kicked him in the head.

 Kayleen M. Hazlehurst

Now it's not the bleakness or despair.
Nor drought, nor overdraft.
But cold envy of the mouths we feed
that breaks a farmer's heart.

To those who walk on paths of gold,
    our critics at the worst,
'Why should the farmers get our help?'
    over lamb and latte, they ask.

For a man whose lost another crop,
    there's little pride about.
It's going broke to save the bull,
    or a government hand me out.

Now it's not the bleakness or despair.
Nor drought, nor overdraft.
But cold envy of the mouths we feed
that breaks a farmer's heart.

(In memory of my father, 2007)

Nora's Sword

AFTER HER MORNING'S shopping, Nora arrived at Mrs Oliver's waterfront residence with her white string bag filled with summer produce. Gertrude Oliver, an artist in her late sixties, had chosen this pleasant spot opposite the seawall at St Heliers Bay when she came out from England in 1920.

The shambling cottage was a haven for Nora. The rooms were replete with reminders of yesteryear—a bow-fronted sideboard in the hall, worn upholstered chairs in the front room, and an oak dining table covered with palettes, rags and tubes of oil paint. Easels leaned in the corner, propping up Gertrude's latest seascape and an emerging portrait of Princess Elizabeth being copied from a photograph. Taking pride of place on the mantelpiece was a picture of her late husband in uniform.

William, an accountant and war poet, was esteemed for his poignant verse published soon after he died in 1915.

Gertrude was impeccably turned out, as usual. She wore long slender dresses, evocative of a former era. This one, in a bohemian maroon, was accompanied by a scarf in cerulean blue and gold. Her translucent skin was dusted with a pinkish powder and her white hair was plaited and coiled at the nape of her neck. Her manners were reminiscent of the cultured middle classes, whose society Nora could only have aspired to during her years in domestic service.

As her first and dearest friend in the new country, Gertrude had become a trusted confidante. Understanding Nora's worries, she always had some kindly remedy.

'Goodness, dear, you look exhausted.' Gertrude reached for Nora's shopping bag and ushered her inside.

'It's the heat, Gertie. My bunions are giving me gyp.'

Gertrude regarded her with calm, grey eyes. 'Have a walk on the beach before our cuppa. A paddle will do marvels for your feet.'

'Sounds nice. Do you mind?'

'Not at all. It will remove the rats from your hair.'

Nora laughed. 'It will, Gertie.'

'Take my sandshoes from the laundry.'

'No, I shan't take them. They don't fit my bunions anymore.'

 Kayleen M. Hazlehurst

'What a shame. Perhaps we should cut little holes on the sides.'

'No point spoiling a good pair of sandshoes. Bare feet will do.'

Bunions were a reality of life. They'd been painfully forcing Nora's big toes further west and east with every passing year. Nothing could be done about them, so there was no point complaining.

'Ta-rah,' Gertrude sung from the front door. 'I'll finish icing our cake. We can have tea the minute you get back from your walk.'

Nora scrunched along the shell path, crossed the quiet street, and negotiated her way down the stone steps of the seawall. Here she removed her sensible lace-ups and immersed her aching feet into the warm sand. She meandered along the bay, moving between the beach and the cooling water. An arc of sunlight reflected off the white cottages and bungalows along the esplanade and heightened the coloured facias of shops.

It wasn't that she wanted to prevent her daughter from 'doing her bit' for her country. It was more that she couldn't bear to see Grace exposed to the world and its wickedness. *How many men are willing to break my daughter's heart? Men with feet of clay, like Charles Harrison. And if the enemy should make its way to New Zealand, what then?*

Nora was seized by a sudden foreboding, as if the sword of Damocles had been hung by its thread over her head.

Her husband had argued in favour. 'Grace will be on a good wicket with the air force, and who knows where that training might lead?'

'It's simply not enough, Henry,' she had responded.

While a mother might anguish, this did not temper her fear of losing the love of her child. *What's a body to do? I'm damned, no matter what course I take.*

Nora's sword slipped further from its knot.

But Auckland Harbour was looking particularly enchanting today and the sea had a way of stilling her inner torments. Young children chirruped beside buckets and spades, smiling up at her when she lingered to admire their sandcastles. White-tipped waves brought squeals from the older ones. Mothers sat watchful with sand scooped against their bare legs, or paddled ankle-deep in the water with towels draped over their arms.

Nora crumpled down on the sand to watch and listen. How much she missed the joyful dependence of little children. Seagulls were not the same thing, but they made fine companions. When one settled nearby, Nora turned gratefully to speak to the bird.

'My daughter is upset with me,' she explained as she ran her fingers through the warm grains.

 Kayleen M. Hazlehurst

The seagull tilted its head, as if to listen.

'It's not that I want to keep Grace a prisoner or to turn her into my slave.' Nora chuckled, recalling Grace's recent accusations. 'Although, being cared for in my old age does sound rather nice. Girls are such a comfort, don't you think?'

The gull ruffled its feathers and burrowed deeper into its hollow.

'It's just … How can I protect her when she's so far away?'

She shaded her eyes to watch the seabirds wheeling left and right above the sparkling waters. Swooping flashes of white, yellow and grey.

When Nora returned to the cottage, she was tranquil again. Tea was served on the round table under the window. On a lace tablecloth, her friend had set out a selection of treats—sugared scones, cucumber sandwiches with their crusts cut off, a Madeira cake smothered in passionfruit icing. At the centre of the table was a familiar china teapot covered with its rainbow cosy. Nora assumed her place by the window while Gertrude took the tapestry-seated chair.

'What a splendid tea, Gertrude. You shouldn't have gone to so much trouble.'

'Something to sustain you, dear. Have you made your decision?'

'No, but I think Grace has already sent in her application.'

'Then it might be out of your hands. We must stand by our children, even when they won't take our advice.'

'Gertie, I am quite besieged. Is it fair to Grace that I worry so?'

'How can we not worry when our families must endure such adversities? These great wars overpower us all.'

'I've brought back the book by Ruth Adam you lent me. The one about spinster teachers.'

'Oh, yes. *I'm Not Complaining*. How did you find it?'

'A sad story. And that's something else the Great War must answer for, leaving a generation of young women all alone in the world without husbands.'

'My dear, don't I know it. But surely Grace is capable of looking after herself?'

'I would prefer that she married. I want grandchildren.'

Gertrude tipped her head towards the side table where she kept a pile of magazines, including the *New Zealand Woman's Weekly* and the monthly edition of the *Mirror*. 'Take a few of those with you today. There are articles about how women are coping without their men.

Some women are finding fulfilment in employment, or in travelling to faraway places. Others have taken up writing books.'

'Frankly, I've done my dash with travelling. Will you ever return to England?' Nora asked, knowing the answer but wanting to reminisce a little about 'Home'.

'No, I shan't go back. I would only be visiting graves. Are there many of your people left?'

'My sister Marjorie, and Aunt May and Uncle Wallace. My brother was wounded in the 1918 Spring Offensive, you'll remember. The Germans were trying to drive a wedge between the British and the French before the Americans arrived.'

The corners of Gertrude's mouth lifted in a bow. 'Oh, I remember it well. They even shelled Paris. My dear, the Parisians were fleeing like rabbits. If the Anzacs hadn't rushed in, bless their hearts, where *would* we have been?'

'All speaking German by now, I shouldn't wonder.' Nora bathed in the sweetness of Gertrude's smile. 'So, you left Britain …'

'As soon as it was safe. I'd been five years without my husband …' Gertrude contemplated the silver-framed photograph on the mantel, her hand suspended above the teapot. 'Dear William was killed so early in the war. Ypres, twenty-sixth of April.' She picked up the teapot and started to pour. 'Mother passed away not long after my two brothers. Grief, I expect, poor thing. The boys died on the same day. Gassed in the trenches.'

Nora gathered her napkin into a peak. 'Such an evil weapon. The injuries, Gertrude. The frightful burns …' When her own brother came home there was little the surgeons could do to repair his face. 'They placed special seats in the parks for the convalescing soldiers, did you hear? That might have happened after you left. The seats were turned away from the path, so people might promenade behind and not stare.'

'That was kind.'

'On some days, Harold went to the parks. Such sad men, all with pinned and tucked clothing. Missing limbs. Wounds that could never be—'

'Poor souls.' Gertrude brushed her napkin with her fingertips.

'Harold sickened after a few months,' Nora continued. 'At first, we suspected typhoid or cholera but in the end he succumbed quite quickly to pneumonia.'

'*Ah*, yes. That terrible pandemic. The influenza went through the soldiers like wildfire.'

The sound of the sea blown in through barely lifting curtains brought a stillness to the room. The ladies sipped their tea, mindful of a war that left two million British women alone as widows or spinsters.

 Kayleen M. Hazlehurst

Nora opened her palms. 'And here they are trying to overrun us again. We sacrificed our husbands and brothers, and now we must send our children after them?'

'We must. For the sake of the grandchildren—'

'And we commit another generation to their deaths—'

'Do they not return to heaven as heroes?' Gertrude's voice wavered, belying her conviction.

'*Really*, Gertrude. How can we be certain of that?'

'We can't. But we would go quite mad if we didn't believe.'

'And these grandchildren,' Nora said, indignant. 'What if their ears are stopped and their eyes cannot see? Will they remember we fought for their freedom?'

'They will remember what they are told. It's up to us to tell them our stories.'

Nora fingered the lace of the tablecloth, her chest heavy with the desire to weep. 'Such a great price, freedom.'

'A great price, indeed.' Gertrude waited, steadying Nora with her attendance.

'So you think I should give my blessing to Grace to join the WAAFs?'

'I think you must. The Auxiliaries will play a supportive role, which is what our men need, surely.'

'What mother would not want to say no? We're all in the same boat, I suppose.'

'We are. Families must do the honourable thing. Give your blessing, Nora dear. It will make everyone feel better.'

'It seems I have no choice.'

With that, Nora's sword sliced through the air and disappeared into a chasm, only inches to her right.

<hr>

(Excerpt: *A Caramel Sky*, Blue Dragonfly Press, Auckland, 2020. Available from bookshops and online booksellers, www.copypress.co.nz)

 Kayleen M. Hazlehurst

Come the Winter—1918

In honour of war widows and lovers

When tardy shapes of tea tree, pine
   and cabbage trees and duck and vine,
do fly afield or arrow point
   are filtered clean or to bone are bleached.

When toitoi flare in seaward crests.
   When driving rains are driven west.
When boats return to wharf or quay
   to shelter there in fired sheds.

In storms …
   that warn …

By sand-locked dune and saffron ray.
   By grass-topped hill and beckoning bay.
By all of me, and all the best
   in longest years and tragic torn.

There, will I wait for you my love …
   Come the winter.

(Love and War, 2010)

A Spring Milking

A briar of shadows
    fall from restless legs.
Gate half-open, where the farmer leans.

A slim herd of Friesians,
    udders swaying full,
wait under a vanilla sky to be called.

Leaves of hardwoods beside the farmhouse
    explode into a fan of rays.
Releasing buds of apple, cherry blossom and plum.

Shafts finger the boards of the milking shed,
    halo the haystack, silhouette the chimney.
Stark and bare against the ingathering light of dawn.

'Come, girls. It is time.'

(In memory of my father, 2021)

 Kayleen M. Hazlehurst

Safer Routes

MIRIAMA WAS SHAKING with trepidation. At any moment her wairua might leap from her chest and race across the ocean in search of her lost children. It was only a mother's hope, people would say, but she was certain one of her sons was alive. She could feel his mauri in the world—he was alive and in peril. Her searing alarm was evidence of this.

She stepped from the garden and walked to the cliff edge to call on the Powers to help the lost and the fallen. Every atua and tūpuna who had ever been a guardian to her family she summoned now to their protection.

Sonny plunged through the water and clawed his way up the bank. These days it seemed he was always wet. This crop-growing area was laced with irrigation ditches that drew water from a myriad of creeks and springs. Huddled under the wooden supports of a bridge, he listened to the rumble of cart wheels and motor vehicles. He preferred to rest under these structures than to risk approaching strangers. Nothing much grew in the shade of bridges, but they provided protection and a dry dirt floor. Once the traffic stopped, he could build a fire to cook a snared duck, a speared trout, or an eel from his traps. Foraging for food was easier near water.

His routine was to sleep half the night, walk south-east under a waning moon, and find a new hideout before sunrise. During the day he hid among the willows and reeds that clustered along the banks of water courses. Here, he drank from streams, sampled water plants and sought game while observing the movements of Germans and Greeks.

This evening he longed for something more comfortable. He leaned into the bank and checked the surrounding fields. Greece was far from a wasteland. Over the centuries every inch of fertile soil had been turned to cultivation. The productive earth of a productive people. Half a mile away a stone building with a flat roof cast a square profile against the darkening horizon. *This might make a good shelter.*

 Kayleen M. Hazlehurst

After a quick appraisal, he gathered his things and sprinted towards the barn.

Api was resting on the back porch, enjoying an ocean breeze, when he heard the patter of canine claws on the footpath. Atarangi must be coming for a visit. Kete and Turi often dashed out to accompany her back to the house. Naughty things. He had even seen them abandon Hēmi in the paddocks when Ata was approaching. The dogs had put 'looking after Atarangi' onto their list of duties since Sonny and Tama left for Europe.

'Uncle Api, are you there?' Ata called, as she came to the seaward side of the house.

'Yep, I'm here.' Api pulled himself up on the divan. A year ago, the doctors had said he might be crippled for life, but Miriama would hear none of it. She wasn't going to let his muscles desert him, she told Api, as she held his feet firmly to the floor. With her massages and medicines, his health had improved. Recently he'd discarded the crutches, finding he could use a walking stick. On good days he watched the milking and did a few jobs.

Atarangi handed him some flowers. 'I brought these for you.'

Api recognised them at once. Blue and orange wild flowers plucked from the dunes, a meeting place for lovers. She reminded him so much of the young Miriama. These precious puhi women who circled around him like the sun and moon, why had he been so blessed?

Kete was leaning against the divan and Api put down his hand to stroke her ears. This little girl was always quiet when her master was in pain.

'I'm glad you've come to walk the dogs. They need cheering up.'

Atarangi crouched to give the dogs a cuddle. 'Hēmi said they've been moping.'

'They're restless, that's all. Don't know what's wrong with them.'

'Yes, you do, Uncle,' she said softly. 'It's what's wrong with us all.'

His eyes blurred and he turned away. 'You go, girlie. Come and see me when you get back. We can have a long talk.'

Wood grated on stone as Sonny heaved open the door. Oak, he judged, by its weight and thickness. The timber was scarred and cracked with age. On entering the barn there was the distinct smell of domestic pig. There were

 Kayleen M. Hazlehurst

no signs of livestock and he assumed the owners had herded them into the hills for safety. The room had a single paned window, intact and dusty. In the corner was a greyed hump of hay. The farmer had been tidy. Grain sacks hung on hooks and the cobble stones were swept clean. Sonny forked a quantity of hay onto the floor and collapsed onto his new bed.

He woke with a beam of sunlight at his feet. It was well past his departure hour. When he looked outside the courtyard was empty except for six or seven chickens. The hens were surviving on garden scratchings and he instinctively searched for a handful of wheat to throw out to them.

During the night a shower of rain had passed over the fields. Droplets glimmered on trees and breaths of vapour rose from orchards. Pressed against the wall, a water barrel was collecting the last of the rainwater as it slid from gutter to pipe. He cupped his hands to drink from the barrel and to wash his face.

Worn-out equipment was scattered on the forecourt. A rusted threshing machine, harnesses and chains, a coil of rope, scoops for measuring grain. He considered the usefulness of a metal rod and a clean tin. If he sharpened the point of the rod with that file on the windowsill it would make a good spear and double up as a cooking skewer. Tin cans were good for boiling water.

A pile of kindling and a short-handled axe lay on a chopping block. The axe was compact, suitable for a woman's hand. An ideal size for a travelling man. Sonny said a brief prayer for the poor farmer and his wife, wishing them well wherever they were and asking forgiveness for the theft of their possessions.

In daylight it was unsafe to make a dash for the river over open fields. But here, at this farm, the surrounding foliage gave him cover to scamper around picking vegetables and fruit, the few eggs he might find, and a bag of grain from leavings in the barn. He had grown weak from hunger and recently felt phlegm gathering in his chest. *Can I risk hiding out here for another day?*

He eyed the chickens. One was lame, skinnier than the rest. With the prospect of roast chook for breakfast, it took him less than a minute to decide to stay.

❦

The marae was wakeful with activity. When it wasn't occupied with ceremonies or speeches, the meeting house was the place where the inner mauri was nourished. The women spread out their crafts on tables and floormats—they stripped flax leaves with blades of mussel shell, pounded and loosened the fibre and dyed it with raurēkau and tānekaha bark—each craftswoman

 Kayleen M. Hazlehurst

inclining her head as they talked and laughed. Cordage was rolled on the women's thighs and pulled taut with strong fingers as they weaved and knotted.

Old friends had a talent for seeing the ridiculous in the smallest notion or incident. In such a manner, the women vied and teased, back and forth. They tossed their heads as another tale was told, their eyes brightened by banter, as they pursued artistic perfection. This was the day the ladies made beautiful things—baskets and mats, capes and cloaks, piupiu and tātua in the colours of red, black and tan.

At Rangitakō, the passion of the widows and senior women for arts and crafts was enhanced by the enthusiasm of the younger ones to learn the traditional songs and dances. Weekend classes were well attended and the aunties had been charged with making the children's costumes.

Atarangi, already a talented craftswoman, was unusual for her age. During these sessions she pestered the older women to teach her the oral traditions, the poetry and proverbs. The craft group ladies were feeling the absence of their youngest member. Touched by recent tragedies, they expressed their concern.

The girl had become vague and distracted since Sonny's death, they said. Some reported seeing her roaming the beach in the mornings, or the dunes at sunset. Others had noticed her lonely figure on the cliff top or walking the hills. Miriama loved Atarangi, and understood they were witnessing a young woman overwhelmed by grief.

Miriama studied the kilt she was weaving for the haka group, smiling up when there was an eruption of laughter in the hall. After the government had delivered its telegrams a space as wide as the universe had opened up inside her. Passing on the traditions was a duty that weighed heavily upon the elders, and nothing was more sacred to a tohunga wahine than the maintenance of rangatira lines. Women were natural custodians of the genealogies. Right marriages must be struck. Arrangements must be made.

There was no doubt about Atarangi Tahiri's lineage. Her father and grandfather were of chiefly stock. Miriama had dearly wanted a Wirima to marry a Tahiri since the birth of her sons. Atarangi had shown high intelligence and a purity of heart, but this girl's mind was a rare and fragile thing. Now her mentor questioned how Atarangi would survive the loss of Sonny, a friendship she had encouraged since childhood.

'Time for tea,' Miriama announced.

It was early for morning tea, but nobody argued. The ladies dropped their work and closed the door against the leaves blown onto the porch. The day was blustery as they strolled arm in arm towards the dining hall. Not unusual

 Kayleen M. Hazlehurst

for mid-winter. It was a chill that was easily dispersed by stoking up the wood range and the attendance of twenty ample bodies.

The two women who'd gone ahead to prepare the refreshments had laid out four teapots, two rows of white cups, and plates of cakes and biscuits.

Years ago, Miriama had swept the young Atarangi under her wing after the loss of her parents. Her decision today wasn't difficult, but first she wanted to discuss it with the women.

Heti and Mata settled at the table with their tea and cakes.

'How is Ata?' Heti asked. 'She hardly speaks to anyone.'

Mata wrinkled her forehead. 'There's a strange look in that one's eyes. She reminds me of Granny King.'

'Granny King died of old age,' Miriama said, recalling the woman's dramatic deterioration following the death of her husband.

'And poor Hine,' insisted Mata. 'Remember poor Hine?'

Not long after her fiancé was killed in the Great War, Hinewai Rawhiti had taken to running along the beach in her nightdress. One night she disappeared. The men launched their boats in the morning to look for the girl. Her torn, half-naked body was found in the limbs of a mangrove tree. Since then the name of the unfortunate one, 'poor Hine', was dredged up at any sign of deviance or madness in the young.

'Hinewai died of drowning,' Miriama rebutted again. 'I expect she slipped and cracked her skull. The tide carried her out and left her in the mangroves.' When she saw the concerned faces around her, she felt ashamed. The women only wanted news of their favourite daughter.

'These wanderings help Atarangi,' she continued. 'Besides, she talks with Api.'

'Her heart is broken ...'

'So young to have lost everything ...'

'She's a lost one, that's for sure ...'

Miriama tapped her fingers on the table while the women consoled each other and shook their heads. When she raised her hand, the nattering stopped. 'I have something to discuss with you ... A proposal.'

'We're listening,' Heti said cautiously, not looking up.

'I think Hēmi and Atarangi should marry.'

Eyes widened. Someone gasped.

'Why?' Mata asked. 'Why do you think they should marry?'

'It is in keeping with the traditions. After a warrior falls in battle his brother may marry his wife. It is the honourable thing to do.'

'That was way back,' objected Heti, 'when men could

     Kayleen M. Hazlehurst

have more than one wife.'

'No-one has married anyone yet,' Mata said.

'Same principle,' Miriama persisted. 'Ka mate te kāinga tahi, ka ora te kāinga rua. When one house dies, a second house lives.'

'What about Winifred?'

'Āe. What about Winifred's house?'

'She's Hēmi's girlfriend.'

'Aren't they engaged or something?'

Miriama shifted uncomfortably in her seat. 'They've waited in case one of them gets sent away.'

'I bet Hēmi will have something to say about this,' Mata protested.

'It's only a suggestion. Winifred has fancy ideas about going to the city.'

'She'll meet some Pākehā fella there ...'

'Or a nice Ngāti Porou boy ...'

'I have a nephew ...'

The women collapsed together in laugher.

'Atarangi needs a strong husband. Someone she can trust.'

Heti frowned. 'Someone *you* can trust, don't you mean, Miriama?'

'If we don't make a good match, we may lose her.'

The aunties looked sorrowfully at each other, as if nothing could be done.

'Good luck making that one stick,' Heti muttered.

❦

Twigs and leaves floated past him or rested beside the bank in whorls of scum. The water here was slow moving. Underwater meadows swayed to the motion of unseen currents. Sonny missed the comforts of the barn, but nothing was going to keep him from his brothers.

'Keep swimming,' he told the rat as it wove through the reeds.

The rodent moved at a relaxed pace between its hunting ground and burrow. Water rats were sleek, accomplished swimmers. Clean-living animals that preferred eating plants, water snails and tadpoles. After an hour of observation, Sonny could trace the domain of his round-faced friend.

In his stew pot the skinny carcass of a waterfowl was simmering. Once cooked, he would consume it, bones and all. He stirred the thin broth with his knife, adding watercress and a handful of leaves that tasted much like spinach. He'd eaten these wild greens before and they hadn't poisoned him. Water lilies, too, were edible. The flower buds, young shoots and seeds. Some plants were bitter, and he wished his mother was here to advise him on which berries and roots he could eat.

 Kayleen M. Hazlehurst

The rat swivelled its ears and paddled to a jut of mud near the burrow. Sonny scratched his beard as he watched the industrious creature popping in and out of the water. Not a bad life for a water rat. He stirred his pot again and glanced over at his companion.

'Don't worry, little kiore. I'm not that desperate.'

Resolved to be friends, they contemplated the blue and gold of the day—the rat on its haunches chewing ends of stalks, Sonny nestled into the dry base of bulrushes—as glassy buds of water congregated against sticks, and sunlight ignited the iridescent wings of dragonflies.

(Excerpt: *Who Disturbs the Kūkupa?* Blue Dragonfly Press, Auckland, 2023. Available from bookshops and online booksellers, www.copypress.co.nz)

Three Poems—1947

1.

What sad spirits, to fall so far from their people.
To lie, forgotten, on some distant soil.
To not take flight over cliff and
dune to that place where
sea kelp swirls and flax leaves twist and knot.

Kātahi ngā wairua pōuri, e hingahin-
ga i tawhiti nei i ō rātou iwi.
Te takoto, te warewaretia nei i runga whenua o iwi kē.
Te kore e rere ā-pari, ā-taipū ki taua wāhi
e āwhio ai te rimurapa, e takawiri
e pūtiki ai te rau harakeke.

2.

Where are the young men
to be inspired by the feats of their ancestors?
Where are the leaders who will shape their lives
by the virtues of the great chiefs?

Kei hea ngā taitama
Hei whakaawe i ngā mahi rangatira ā ō rātou tūpuna?
Kei hea ngā kaiarataki hei tauira i te oranga
me ngā horomata o te rangatira rongo nui?

 Kayleen M. Hazlehurst

3.

So, little flycatcher.
Will you come out to boldly challenge me
when I approach the place of Hinenuitepō?
Or will I be renewed like the moon and restored to life?

Nō reira e te kaihopu ngaro iti.
Ka māia tō puta mai ki te takitaki i ahau
I ahau ka tata atu nei ki te kāinga o Hinenuitepō?
Ka whakaorahia mai anō rānei pērā i te marama hōu?

Will you laugh and dance
when I come alive in the sunlight?
Will you love me when I come to you at dawn?
Hah! And they said Māui would never return!

Ka kata ka kanikani rānei koe
Ina ora mai anō au ā te whitinga o te rā?
Ka aroha mai koe ina hoki atu au
ki a koe i te ata hāpara?
Ha! Me tā rātou kī mai, e kore a Māui e hoki mai!

(Excerpt: *Who Disturbs the Kūkupa?* Blue Dragonfly Press, Auckland 2023. English to Māori translations by Rahera Shortland, translations editor Basil Keane. Available from bookshops and online booksellers, www.copypress.co.nz)

Louise

1992

A KID OF about five came to her doorstep on a scooter. 'Have you seen Rashid?' he asked. It was nearly dark and the boy's sixteen-year-old brother had gone missing after school the night before. A few minutes later a policeman arrived. The headmaster had suggested Louise Hammond be paid a visit. Yes, she was a friend of the Indian couple who ran the corner grocery store, but she didn't buy the explanation.

This fine spring day had started with choir practice at the community hall. Choristers met every second Friday, except at Easter. Sessions with the choirmaster and pianist ran between nine and ten-thirty, followed by a morning tea. Louise never missed it. The girls at her shop had hastened their manageress away, saying how fabulous she looked. Louise was the first local to wear vintage fashions and took extra care on choir days. Frocks unearthed from their mothers' era tickled the older women.

'Come in, Sergeant,' she said, stepping back. 'And here is me in my pink dressing gown and fluffy slippers about to wash my hair.'

There were no knickers or hosiery hanging on the clothes horse beside the bay window. She had checked. Yet, Sergeant Ronald Winfield still looked uncomfortable standing in her living room. The man wasn't very broad-minded.

It wasn't the first time the teen had crept away from his family to be with his mates. As the officer droned on about the worried parents, asking who would pick up the potatoes and cabbages for the pub, Louise drifted into thoughts about her new life.

Two years ago she had moved to 9 Shepherds Lane in Limetree. The estate agent had been right. It *was* a 'picturesque country town'. Here she could find peace among the pastured fields, the vacant scrubland and forested hills. She'd heard rural people were more accepting. Frankly, she was tired of the city flimflam and prejudice. She had made mistakes. The antique shop she'd purchased in the village generated poor returns. Few customers were interested in its stock of old furniture and bric-a-brac—glass vases, china teacups, porcelain

     Kayleen M. Hazlehurst

figurines, painted miniatures and pre-loved jewellery. But by adding a range of vintage clothes, she had started to turn things around.

The sopranos and altos got behind her, bringing their out-of-date frocks into the shop, rather than taking them to the flea markets. Florals, pleats, polka dots and stripes. *Harper's Bazaar* panache. Treasures that made customers shriek when they found them.

She tossed off a little laugh. 'So we are on another hunt for the naughty Rashid, Sergeant?'

The policeman did a quick recce of the room. Majeed studied her with large black eyes and smiled when he heard the word 'naughty'.

'What about you, Majeed?' she asked. 'Any idea where your brother is?'

He dolefully shook his head.

'Did Mum ask you to fetch me?'

The boy nodded.

Winfield seemed impatient to get home to his dinner. A member of the choir himself, he would turn up on occasions to exercise his baritone vocal cords.

'I didn't see you at the hall this morning,' Louise said.

'Didn't I tell you? I was out looking for a lost teenager.'

'Sorry, he's not here. Would you like me to talk to Mr and Mrs Bashi? Take this one back to his parents?' She tilted her head towards the child.

'I can drive you, if you like. You okay with walking home?'

'Main Street is well lit,' she answered.

'By the way, where were you today?'

'After choir I went to the shop. Where else would I be?'

'Anyone see you?'

'Don't be ridiculous, Ronny. Of course they did.'

'Just doing my job ... Don't leave town without telling me.'

She lifted her shoulders in a sigh. 'Why would I leave? I have a business to run.'

Some months earlier her assistants, Jenny and Gail, had concocted the idea of a boutique café. A tearoom with a bric-a-brac ambience. Louise liked the idea. Home cooking with Mum had filled many happy hours of childhood. There was enough money to install a modest kitchen and she let the eatery flow through the shop.

The old standbys of bangers and mash, sausage rolls, pie and peas, and fish and chips were put on the menu for any stray men, but the main attractions for women were the finger sandwiches, smoked fish savouries, devilled eggs and a selection of 'Grandma's sweet treats'. High teas were back in vogue.

A TV special showcased Louise's Vintage Café and overnight Limetree became 'charming'. Friends came to exchange recipes and to share tiny versions of melting moments, chocolate Afghans, Madeira cake and scones with strawberry jam and cream. In keeping with the theme, a few ladies wore fifties twinsets with flared skirts and rayon scarves. Tourists who stopped in for the new eating experience went on to explore the local shops. It had been good for the whole town and the sergeant knew it.

Louise tightened her dressing gown and edged towards the hall. 'Give me a minute to dress.'

'I'll meet you at the car. Come on, kid. How would you like a ride in a police car?'

She raked through her bedroom closet. Parents of a lost child required something sedate and she settled on the dark-blue linen. A Betty Carol fold-over with large buttons. She adjusted her wig in the long mirror and ran her hands over her slim hips. At forty-two she wasn't frumpy. She drew on her coat, hesitating before discarding the pearl brooch.

During the drive she told the policeman which songs the choir had practised that morning, neither adult wanting to discuss their worst fears in front of an anxious little boy.

'We did a bit of scat. Listened to a tape of Ella Fitzgerald and Mel Tormé. It was fun.'

Ronny shook his head. 'I'm sorry I missed that.'

Boy and scooter were dismounted on the pavement outside Bashi's Groceries.

'Thanks for the lift,' Louise said. 'I'll let you know if I learn anything.' Immigrant families were not keen on talking to the police, even about misplaced relatives.

A lady in a blue sari and white apron, looking all of her fortyish years, came to the front step. She appeared relieved to see them but presented a stern face. 'Majeed, I asked you to bring me Louise, not to bother the policeman for a ride home.'

'That was my fault,' Louise said. 'Majeed and Sergeant Winfield arrived at my house about the same time. He offered us a ride and I accepted. Hope you don't mind.'

The woman shrugged. 'Dinner is in the kitchen, Majeed. Hurry now, Dad will need your help.' She waved them inside, then asked Louise, 'Why was the policeman visiting?'

'He's been making enquiries. I'm sure he thinks I'm hiding Rashid in my back room ... Silly man.'

'Well, we don't think you are. Come in, dear. We must talk.'

'Have you heard anything yet?'

'Nothing.' Mrs Bashi lifted her apron to wipe her eyes. 'They think Rashid has run away, but we fear someone has stolen him.'

     Kayleen M. Hazlehurst

'Goodness.' She was ushered into the family room behind the kitchen.

'You will take us seriously, won't you, Louise?'

'Certainly, I will. Has someone been threatening you?'

'We'll wait for Sabat. Can I offer you a cup of tea? It's my special blend.'

'That would be wonderful, Mrs Bashi.'

'Please, call me Aesha. I have prepared samosas. Fried vegetable dumplings. Do you like them?'

Louise removed her coat. 'I love anything Indian.'

Tea came on a trolley with matching cups and teapot. 'Next time you must come to dinner. That's a nice dress. What is the material?'

'Linen. You can touch the fabric if you like. I put it on when I can't think of anything else to wear.'

Aesha's eyelashes fluttered, as if she was struggling with a question. 'Have you always worn women's clothes?'

'I wore a three-piece suit to my office in Auckland.'

'Your job must have been very important.'

'I was a financial adviser. Sadly, I saw the worst of humanity in that work. There's too much greed in the city.'

Aesha stopped pouring their tea. 'So, you moved to Limetree and became a woman?' she said, her voice rising slightly.

Louise brooded for a moment, then went on. 'When I was a child, my sister, Kimberly, used to dress me up like a doll. I liked the attention. She could be cruel when I looked like a boy. I guess she wanted a little sister.'

'That was very unfair.'

'I have cross-dressed on and off most of my life.'

'Well, I don't see the harm.'

'Some people don't like me because of it.'

'Never mind. People don't like us because of the colour of our skin, or our religion, or because our clothes are different.'

'I'm sorry. That must be painful.'

'In India we embraced our differences. Our lives were much more vibrant and colourful.'

'I understand.' Louise knew the need for vibrancy and colour.

'In Kerala, the state we are from, Hindu men dress as women during the Kottankulangara Festival in honour of the goddess, Bhagavathy. A thousand men put on make-up and their brightest saris to please the goddess and to seek her blessings.' Aesha smiled. 'Oh Louise, I wish you could see them …'

Mr Bashi came in and crumpled into the chair beside her.

'Long day?' Louise asked.

 Kayleen M. Hazlehurst

'I've been up since five. How are you, my dear? Your business is flourishing?'

'I've made some progress.'

'Good. We all benefit when our neighbours prosper.'

'I've been telling her about the temple festival, Sabat.'

'Ah, yes. The night when ordinary men are transformed into demure goddesses, each bringing to the temple their own offerings and sacredness. It's a wonderful ceremony. Crowds visit Kerala for the festival. There is always an elephant.'

Louise laughed. 'Only in India ...'

'Sabat was a supplicant before we were married.'

'Why, Aesha, I think you are blushing.'

Aesha's smile was coy. 'Some devotees are very beautiful.'

Louise sat forward to sip her tea. 'And many devotees are young men?'

'Yes,' Aesha said softly.

'May I ask what blessings you beseeched from your Devi, Sabat?'

'I was seeking a wife and good fortune.'

'As young men do.'

Aesha glanced over as she attended to Sabat. 'When you are not Louise, what is your name? What did your mother call you?'

'She named me Lewis.'

'And sometimes you dress as a man?'

Louise chuckled. 'When I'm washing my car.'

Sabat lowered his cup and wiped his moustache. 'I should like to meet this Lewis fellow. Does he like fishing?'

'Not particularly, but he'll watch a game of cricket with you.'

It was late before she got away from her friends. The small talk about cross-dressing goddesses was intriguing, with or without the elephant, but what interested her most were the couple's thoughts about their lost son and why they expected to hear something soon.

To get home she had to walk past a row of small shops and The Ploughman, a traditional country pub. *If only I'd brought my wheels.*

She had two vehicles. An '86 Holden Gemini she'd bought cheaply in Auckland before the model was discontinued, and a dishevelled truck she'd inherited with the antique shop. She enjoyed driving the battered pickup—the way every bump and curve in the road tethered her to the environment.

Even with her coat wrapped tight, her heart pounded and her ankles wobbled in her heels as catcalls and taunts were hurled at her by drunken patrons outside the hotel.

'Hello, darling, want a date? I'm available.'

Louise heard men laughing, and an engine revving-up

  Kayleen M. Hazlehurst

as she hurried away. She turned onto the dim path leading to Shepherds Lane, avoiding the dark driveways and hedges. Those men at the pub knew who she was. Many had come to the café to stare at her during the day. By the time she got home she was shaking.

On Saturday afternoon she visited the police station.

'You must make Rashid your top priority, Sergeant. People are getting twitchy.'

Neville and Lance, two young constables at their desks, pretended not to be listening.

'That's what I'm doing,' Ronald whispered over the counter. 'Anyway, what do you know about runaway kids?'

'More than you think. And he may not be a runaway.'

The policeman regarded her with cool grey eyes. 'Maybe one of *your* folk grabbed him?'

'What do you mean *my* folk?'

He tipped his head three times and smirked.

Louise gave him a silent glare.

Winfield turned red. 'Never mind. Auckland Central have a photo. They will be trawling the city, checking out the streets and sleazy clubs.'

'Rashid could have joined an Indian dancing troupe. He might be heading for Bollywood as we speak.'

'Oh, I doubt ...' Winfield raised his eyebrows. 'Really?'

'It's one of the parents' theories. Have you considered looking closer to home? I don't feel safe here at the moment, myself. A few men have been getting nasty.'

'What do you expect?' He waved his hand over her dress.

'So I'm the architect of some boy-snatching ring between Limetree and Auckland?'

'You said it, not me ... Are you?'

'I don't have any criminal leanings, Ronny. But you already know that.'

'Yeah, I've checked you out. Sorry those bastards have been bothering you.' He looked apologetic ... 'I have a dog.'

'What?'

'Useless thing, sent to me last week from the Police Dog Section. Spectacular dropout from training school. Frightened of his own shadow.'

'What are you saying?'

'The mutt needs a home ... You need protection ... How about taking him in until I get something sorted?'

She paused. 'Is the animal friendly?'

'Love ya to death. Too nice for police work. Doesn't want a bar of chasing villains, hates searching for drugs, and is none too keen on cadaver detection.'

'I don't blame him... I suppose I could take him to the café.'

Neville lifted his head. 'You won't have to buy a thing.'

Lance got to his feet. 'I could drop him off with his stuff before dinner.'

'How much stuff?'

'Just a bed and a few toys.'

'All right. I'll give your wretched dog a home until you find Rashid. As long as you lot put your backs into the search.'

'Teamwork. That's the spirit.' The sergeant almost sounded like he believed his own rhetoric.

She turned to go, feeling railroaded. Glancing back, she saw the whole station had come up smiles. 'What kind of dog is it?'

'Black Labrador.'

'Bit of a sook but has a bark like a foghorn.'

'Would scare away any prowler.'

'Thanks a bunch.'

Winfield held open the door. 'I reckon Bentley will suit you down to the ground.'

'Bentley. That's his name?'

'Yeah.'

'Sounds enormous.'

The canine arrived an hour later with his paraphernalia, including two bowls and a box of dog food. Louise and the Labrador stood in the kitchen staring at each other. He was an impressive animal, about eighteen months old. Black coat, so shiny ducks could use him as a water slide. Solid neck and shoulders. Broad head. Not the sort of pet a lady in a pencil skirt should be seen towed along by. As his name suggested, Bentley was a finely-tuned machine who just wanted to run.

❦

Lewis rose early and put on his jeans and pullover. After a man-sized Sunday breakfast for them both, he grabbed his mackintosh and boots from the porch.

'Come on, boy. Get in the truck.'

By the time he mounted the driver's seat, the dog was settled on the passenger side as if he owned the spot, with his eyes fixed straight ahead.

'There's a walk not far from here. You'll like it. A forest with lots of room to explore. You'd better behave, else it'll be the park from now on.'

Bentley lolloped his tongue around his lips, spraying saliva on the glove compartment.

'Lovely.' Lewis reached for a cloth to wipe the animal's mouth. 'I know, you're excited. Cooped up all week at the station, were you?'

They turned off the highway and continued on a side road for a few minutes before pulling into a carpark.

A *Public Walkway* sign had been nailed to the gate post, accompanied by a map, and the request to *Please stay on the path*.

Lewis was familiar with Winchester Forest. A creek could be followed down to the road if a person got lost. He tightened the laces of his hiking boots and shouldered his rucksack. He had only packed emergency items—a medical kit, a knife and rope, a trowel and some toilet paper, a water bottle, supply of nuts and raisins, and two dog biscuits.

He had also brought one of Rashid's shirts provided by the boy's parents.

He had stopped in again at the corner store before Saturday closing.

'Hello, I'm Lewis.'

Aesha had taken a step back, this being the first time she'd seen him in men's clothing. Without the wig, he had short brown hair that was greying at the temples.

Sabat grasped his extended hand. 'Glad to meet you, Lewis. This is a very great pleasure.'

'Will you stay a while?' Aesha asked, having recovered herself.

'Sorry, not this evening. I have a house guest.'

After explaining he was caring for a rescue dog, the mother had rushed off to find an item of clothing.

'Get his sports shirt,' Sabat called after her. 'The one he kept in his school locker,' then he turned to Lewis. 'Will you do some detective work for us, my friend?'

Aesha came back from the bedroom in tears. 'Please, Lewis,' she begged as she handed over the shirt. 'Please help us find Rashid before it's too late.'

The forest park was always quiet on Sunday mornings. Bentley was scratching at the truck door to get out. The animal raced through the gate and left the path with Lewis following. After vanishing for a few minutes, Bentley rocketed back and bounced off his legs.

'Hey, watch it!'

The black dog dropped his bum into top gear and streaked off into a loop. Lewis trotted towards a stand of kauri and tōtara, wondering if he would ever see the animal again. High-pitched yelping indicated Ben had fastened onto a rabbit trail. There was no point trying to catch a speeding dog. Either the rabbit would outrun him or the trail would go cold. Lewis checked his watch and sat down on a log to wait. In a short time, he heard panting.

He whistled to the dark shape weaving through the trees. 'Over here, Ben. Come, boy.'

Bentley came padding towards him, carrying something in his mouth.

     Kayleen M. Hazlehurst

'What have you got there?'

As the dog neared him, he realised it was the frayed sleeve of a chequered shirt with the clawed bones of a hand.

Limetree Police Station called in reinforcements. Three experienced handlers with their detection dogs flew in via the airfield north of the town.

Lewis and Bentley showed the team the general area. They had scoured the forest earlier but *old Clueless* couldn't remember where he had found the bones. While the professionals did a wide sweep, Bentley whined and pulled at his lead.

'Quiet, boy. You had your chance.'

It was midday before the police located the human remains.

During a three hour search the bystanders at the entrance to the forest had grown to a small crowd. Clustered behind the orange tape, they wanted to know why murderers were burying bodies so near to their peaceful village.

The Bashis were assured the body could not have been their missing son. Decomposition confirmed the bones had lain there for some time, and Mrs Bashi said Rashid had never owned a chequered shirt. With no other missing persons on his books, Sergeant Winfield was at a loss to come up with an identity. 'Forensics should help us with that,' he muttered, shaking his head.

Auckland Central Police wanted to be sure no more bodies were buried in the park and the detection team was instructed to widen its search. Bentley was not invited to attend the next day. It was probably for the best. Being left out the first time had made the beast mopey.

❦

Louise read up on Labradors. Daily walks and games of fetch and tug-of-war were supposed to build confidence in a dog, but Ben had other problems. Fireworks, backfiring cars, being left alone for more than five minutes. A clap of thunder had him wedged behind a lounge chair with his pupils thrust sideways and the whites of his eyes reflecting spotlights off the ceiling.

From his behaviour it was clear Ben was empathetic. At the café he would lick a crying child or nuzzle a sad grown-up. If they were ever burgled, Louise was certain Bentley would help the thief carrying out the silverware.

One speculation about Rashid's disappearance kept circling back. In any domestic situation a relative was often suspected and it came to light that Sabat had a disgruntled older brother, who had arrived in New Zealand on the same wave of migration.

Zahir owned a successful Indian restaurant in central Auckland. Aesha and Sabat were particularly reticent when speaking about Rashid's uncle, and his rise to affluence. Louise guessed he dealt in more than curries. Maybe his booths were convenient places for seedier transactions. Businessmen with their fingers in the wrong pots, money laundering, get-rich-quick schemes, illegal gambling, prostitution and the growing drug trade. While one shady relative in the city might not hurt an honest, hard-working couple with a small country store, this landscape suddenly changed when she discovered Zahir bore a grudge.

The family story had come out on the Friday night. Back in Kerala the first wife of the older brother had died young, having failed to bear him a son. Three years later he and his second wife were afflicted by similar misfortune. Some time before the two families migrated, the second sister-in-law gave birth at the same maternity hospital as Aesha. Sons were born hours apart to the two women.

During the night one child passed away. Zahir berated the nursery. Maddened with grief, he alleged they had switched babies. There was a bitter struggle and the stricken father had to be dragged away by police. He had never forgiven Sabat and Aesha.

Relating the event, Aesha had lifted her hands in an appeal to Louise. 'Rashid will be seventeen next month. If his uncle offers him a job, and he accepts, the authorities will never challenge it.'

'Our son would never be seduced by Zahir's riches,' Sabat insisted. 'He's being held against his will. Now the boy is grown my brother thinks he can steal him from us. He has been plotting this for years.'

These were wild ideas, yet they sounded plausible. 'Would Zahir have kidnapped the boy himself?'

Sabat rammed down his fist. 'You can bet he sent others to do his dirty work.'

'They took Rashid on his way home from school,' Aesha sobbed. 'He'll be so frightened.'

'Then it is definitely abduction. No matter what age he is. Do you want me to tell the police?'

Sabat shifted forward. 'The kidnappers will cut his throat if we involve the police!'

Aesha uttered a cry and put her hand to her mouth.

'Don't worry,' Louise had said, reaching out her hand. 'I'll make some discreet enquiries. It's amazing what people will tell you over a cup of coffee and a free lump of coconut ice.'

The police were conducting their enquiries house to house. It wasn't every day a child in school uniform was snatched off the streets of Limetree. Rashid would have resisted. There'd have been a struggle.

Louise's first port of call was the café. At closing time, she told Jenny and Gail about her mission to find the missing youth and the girls swung right in behind her.

'We must recruit the choir ladies,' Gail said, as she washed the last dishes.

Jenny tidied away the cups. 'Should we invite them for morning tea?'

'I don't see why not.' Louise agreed, a meeting was the quickest way to launch an investigation. 'We'll make extra pikelets.'

Jenny collapsed into giggles against the sink. 'Twenty old ducks asking around will unearth more information than those police officers ever can.'

'Don't let Sergeant Winfield hear you say that.'

'Sergeant Winfield couldn't find his necessities on his wedding night,' Gail said dryly, sending them screeching into the next room to straighten the tables.

The choir ladies arrived at 10 am. Each had expressed a concern for the Bashi family and a morning tea was an excellent opportunity for a natter. Three of the women had sons in produce delivery. Two daughters catered for the school. There were friends who were daily shoppers. Grandchildren, too, had sharp eyes. They would ask if anyone had seen anything suspicious—a lurking vehicle, men acting funny.

After work, while they waited for incoming intelligence, Louise and Bentley went to hunt for clues. Their strolls between the corner store and the school gates produced nothing. She stopped at the hairdresser's for the latest gossip, then the bakery where local children bought doughnuts, all to no avail.

Cruising homeward in the truck she tried to imagine where criminals might lie low for three or four days. The police were doing spot-checks along the highway. Nearby farms were on the alert. The sea required a boat, but coastal destinations had many eyes.

That only left ... 'The airfield, Ben! Why didn't I think of it?'

Bentley answered with a resounding 'Woo-woo' and sloshed his tongue round his lips.

Lewis threw his wig on the seat, wiped off his lipstick, and did a one-eighty outside the police station. He took out his mobile phone, although he still hadn't got used to using the clunky brick.

'I know where they are, Jenny. I'm going out to the airfield. Can you tell Gail?'

 Kayleen M. Hazlehurst

'Look for a van with two men,' was her urgent response. 'That's what the ladies are saying. Plain white. No signs or markings.'

'Right.'

There were two more hours of daylight. Plenty of time to reach the site before sunset. Further north, the unmanned strip was being used by recreational pilots, aerial top dressers, medical helicopters and for police emergencies.

As he neared the turn-off, he glanced at the highway through his rear-view mirror. On the range he could see flashing lights. The girls had alerted the police. A dark line of other vehicles trailed behind. It looked like half the population of Limetree was coming to the rescue.

'Damn it!'

Lewis turned onto the gravel road and stopped. He snatched up his T-shirt and jeans from the back seat, changed his clothes, and shoved his feet into a solid pair of sandshoes.

When he reached the airfield, he stopped to check for human activity. A cluster of storage units and sheds stood at the edge of the strip. Parked outside one was an unmarked white van.

'Gotcha!'

'*Mm-m-m-m*,' said Bentley.

Lewis slipped the truck into gear, estimating he had ten minutes before the cavalry arrived. As the truck rolled forward, its tyres scrunching over the stony ground, the dog became tense.

'Okay, boy,' he said, reaching under his seat to retrieve Rashid's shirt. 'Sniff this.'

As he drew in behind the building a deep rumble emitted from Bentley's chest. Either the dog didn't like the situation, or he'd caught a scent.

'Good boy. Stay here.'

Lewis crept to the corner of the shed and crouched down. In the window facing the airfield he saw a flickering light, perhaps a candle. Two men were conversing rapidly in what he guessed was Hindi and a younger voice was answering in English.

'No. I want to go home!'

'Shut your mouth!'

He heard a crack and a thump. Someone had been hit. Had fallen. The boy was calling for his mother, making Lewis clench his fists.

Out of the crimson clouds came the buzz of a descending aircraft. A sliding door scraping on metal was his cue to depart. He rolled to the side and darted behind the shed. Small planes could land, turn around, and take off in minutes. This one was already lining up its headlights.

In the seconds it took Lewis to get back into his pickup, the men had bundled a blanketed figure out of the shed and were running with him across the field.

'Hang on, Ben. This will be rough.'

He spun the vehicle onto the grass. The kidnappers were just yards from the plane, shouting to each other as the truck bore down on them. They shoved their victim on board while the pilot revved the engines and reset the wing flaps.

As the aircraft started to move the last thing Lewis saw was Rashid's desperate face at the plane window. Something inside him broke, seeing that boy so overpowered.

'Agh-h-h!'

Lewis dropped a gear and booted the accelerator, sending up a cloud of dust. He pelted along the airstrip until he was parallel with the horrified face of the pilot. Lewis smiled coolly, drew his finger across his neck, and pointed for the plane to pull over.

Behind him a racket had broken out as police and other vehicles joined in the chase. Sirens, and twenty carloads of screaming citizens were too much for Bentley. The dog stuck his head out the window and bayed like a basset hound.

The pilot didn't call his bluff, seeing the maniac beside him was about to throw a truck under his wheels.

The plane coughed and slowed to a halt as the police and the rest of the snarling pack surrounded it like a cornered hog.

The parents came over as the police led three men away in handcuffs.

Aesha was in tears. 'Oh, thank you, dear. Thank you.' The dazed youngster beside her nodded vigorously.

Sabat gripped Lewis' hand. 'May all the goddesses smile their blessings on your life, my dear friend.'

Gail and Jenny with a group of fascinated locals watched on.

Jenny placed her hand on his chest. 'Lewis, eh?' She grinned. 'Don't you scrub up lovely?'

(Excerpt: *The Antique Chef.* A novella. Blue Dragonfly Press, Auckland 2023. Available from bookshops and online booksellers, www.copypress.co.nz)

 Kayleen M. Hazlehurst

Last Plane to Paradise

A strapping policewoman seizes a child's scooter.
    From the handlebars, she separates the stem.
    From the stem, she detaches the deck.
The youngster looks up with a brave face, not crying.

The woman sprays sanitiser onto cloths.
    She wipes down all the pieces,
    with barely a word or a smile.
Then the chariot is restored to the parents and child.

At a table, two soldiers and four police tick off names.
    The space is suffused with disquiet. An edginess.
    No jovial banter. No sassy ribbing or idle gossip.
Strangers were not to breach this partitioned divide.

I watch briefly, not wanting to stare. Quarantine.
We have come home on the last plane to paradise.

I find myself admiring our frontline workers.
    Their shared commitment. Their focus of minds.
    Similar to the fighters of last summer's firestorms.
They will do the job, even if their own homes are burning.

 Kayleen M. Hazlehurst

The lift takes me to an underground carpark.
     Concrete walls, closed doors, cobwebbed ventilation.
     An officer with a glowing face checks off my name.
A fine-looking fellow, twenty years my junior.

'How long may I walk around?'
     'Exercise for thirty minutes. Don't talk to anyone.'
'Thank you,' I smile and breathe in the cloistered air.
     He grins back. 'No worries, Darl',' he says,
and his words fall at my feet like a bouquet of flowers.

(Paradise Lost Series, 2020)

King Tides

In honour of Ukraine

King Tides:
  A maritime warning.

Caution. King Tides may occur.
  Unusual heights of water.
Coastal surges in summer.
  Winter waves from cyclones and storms.

The Sun may have an influence,
  and the natural pull of Earth.
At night while we are sleeping
  under elliptical orbits of Moon.

Tidelines to many are familiar.
  Oceans appear our friends.
Yet the height of water can vary.
  King Tides will catch us unprepared.

When the purple sheen absorbs us,
  as we rest entitled on our beds,
we may fail to throw up the ramparts
  against famine, war and disease.

(Paradise Lost Series, 2022)

     Kayleen M. Hazlehurst

The Citadel

A young mother holds a child close to her chest.
  Around her, bombs are falling.
    Her people are starving. Their homes in ruins.
Threads of modesty veil her hair at the Prophet's behest.

The Great Pretender has entered the Citadel.
  Vainglory sits upon the Throne of Christ.
    Moses has abandoned the Promised Land.
Leaving them to their golden idols and vengeance of fire.

The seventh Adam has fled Eden.
  Abraham has taken his flocks to the hills.
    Their robes glimpsed among the oranges and olives.
On the slopes of the Holy Mountain, they have built a
  place of Peace.

Yet still, the bombs are falling.
  The souls of the innocent ascend as angels.
    The atoms of the guilty are bound to the dust.

Worshippers issue mantras in their own defence.
  While the world stands by and weeps,
    And Earth grows weary of their feet.

(Paradise Lost Series, 2025)

Ode to a Chestnut Tree

Not once I'd climbed that chestnut tree and felt
the prick of dead and splitting chestnut balls,
now wedged and caught between its forking arms.
But always spritely, as some nesting bird,
my tiny feet had conquered all its traits.

It seemed to sit upon that hill like a fat
and swarthy man. Although its girth was thick
and round, its height was rather low. It was
with caution that I trod, barefoot, across
its shade before, to reach the trunk and climb.

For all around a moat of fallen nuts,
like soldiers stood, to ward off climbers
with their Gothic ball and spike.
Most of my friends, to save the pain,
would choose some other tree.

Only the brave and valiant knight, as I,
would cross and join it in its place. Stop a
moment. Lean to pluck away the thorns
I missed this time from tender toes,
before ascending my dark and wooden tower.

 Kayleen M. Hazlehurst

That was when I felt the prick of dead
and splitting chestnut balls, now wedged
between its forking arms. Then I would choose.
I would choose one branch as if I chose a path
upon a fork of life to seek reward.

Entering there, its thick and giddy head,
crowned with the lush of green and gold,
my coronation was more than heavy leaves
and yet unfallen, spikey chestnut balls.
It was a knight's reward, a kingly place.

Upon my throne I'd swing my feet to view
the reason why such steady guard was kept.

Wrapped in a glistening summer's day
the valley below our crest spread out
a carpet of royal greens and moistened hues,
of grass and fields and trees. Above them all,
we reigned. The king, the castle, moat and throne.

(Childhood poem first composed 1961, aged 11 years)

Kayleen Hazlehurst was born in Warkworth, North Auckland, and began to write stories and poetry as a child growing up on a farm beside the Mahurangi River. Her research and advocacy as an anthropologist took her to remote communities in  the Canadian Arctic, United States, Australia and New Zealand. She later retrained as a medical herbalist and naturopath.

Kayleen's work reflects an empathy with nature and a passionate interest in social issues. Her two recent novels are family sagas of love and war. *A Caramel Sky* is about the air defence and intelligence missions of the Royal New Zealand Air Force, set in the Pacific Islands and the Home Front during the Pacific War. *Who Disturbs the Kūkupa?* is a story of courage and survival during the ANZAC campaigns in Greece, Crete and Italy, particularly those of the 28th Māori Battalion.

She now divides her time between New Zealand and Australia, where she has families.